Mischief & Metaphors

&

Mischief & Metaphors

Essaying a Life

Eileen M. Cunniffe

with artwork by
Rose Marie Cunniffe

SHANTI ARTS PUBLISHING
BRUNSWICK, MAINE

Mischief & Metaphors
Essaying a Life

Copyright © 2023 Eileen M. Cunniffe

All Rights Reserved
No part of this document may be reproduced or transmitted in any form or by any means without prior written permission of the publisher, except in the case of brief quotations embodied in critical reviews.

Published by Shanti Arts Publishing

Designed by Shanti Arts Designs

Cover and interior images are the work of
Rose Marie Cunniffe and are used with her permission.
Cover image is *Big Plans*, acrylic/collage on blueprint and canvas.

Shanti Arts LLC
193 Hillside Road
Brunswick, Maine 04011
shantiarts.com

Printed in the United States of America

ISBN: 978-1-956056-79-2 (softcover)

Library of Congress Control Number: 2023933718

*For the always-inspiring
and ever-expanding tribe
known as Club 441*

Contents

Acknowledgments	9
Preface	13
Everything I Need to Know I'm Still Learning from Mary Richards	17
Trouble-Making	31
Sibling Revelry	35
Stitches in Nine	41
Necessary Things	45
The Great Butter Caper of Chartres	51
Ghost Story	61
Dear Phillies	67
Independence Day	73
Shifting Landscapes	77
Happy Groundhog Day	89
Famous Pink Raincoat	99
Sifting Through It	101
Interior Spaces	113
Santa Fe Stories	119
That Breathless Charm	129
Consignments	135
Somebody Almost	145
Revision, Like Launching a Marble Boat	151
When the Bough...	157
Van Morrison and Me	161
Dear Santa Fe	163
Special Delivery	169
The Writing on the Wall	173
The Sound of a Flinch	179
Happy Hour	185
About the Author	191

Acknowledgments

The author extends her gratitude to the editors of the following publications in which these essays first appeared:

Air: A Radio Anthology (Books by Hippocampus): "Stitches In Nine," 2019

Ascent: "Sifting Through It," 2011

Bluestem Magazine: "Everything I Need to Know I Am Still Learning from Mary Richards," 2016

Door Is a Jar: "Special Delivery," 2018

Emrys Journal: "Shifting Landscapes," 2013

Emrys Journal Online: "When the Bough," 2018

Funny Pearls: "Dear Santa Fe," 2020

Gravel: "Happy Hour," 2019

Hippocampus Magazine: "Dear Phillies," 2012

Lowestoft Chronicle: "Independence Day," 2015

The Mark Literary Review: "Happy Groundhog Day," 2021

Neighbors: A Crack the Spine Themed Anthology: "The Sound of a Flinch," 2020

Philadelphia Stories: "That Breathless Charm," 2009

Prime Number Magazine: "Ghost Story," 2012

The Ravensperch: "The Writing on the Wall," 2018

Still Point Arts Quarterly: "Somebody Almost," 2019

Stone Voices: "Santa Fe Stories," 2014

Superstition Review: "Consignments," 2012; "Interior Spaces," 2013; "Revision, Like Launching a Marble Boat," 2016; "Trouble-Making," 2015; "Van Morrison and Me," 2012

The Voices Project: "Famous Pink Raincoat," 2016

Windmill: The Hofstra Journal of Literature & Art: "Sibling Revelry," 2017.

Wild River Review: "The Great Butter Caper of Chartres," 2007

Wild Violet Magazine: "Necessary Things," 2013

Preface

THIS COLLECTION OF LINKED ESSAYS EXPLORES IDENTITY and experience through three distinct—though often overlapping—lenses: work, family, and travel. The essays come in many shapes and sizes, as do our days and our occasional flashes of insight. They are arranged not-quite-chronologically because life unfolds in a spiral, not a straight line. Some essays capture one brief episode, while others move back and forth in time over several years. For me, the essay form is an invitation to inspect, make sense of, document, and sometimes celebrate my life and the lives of those around me. The cast of characters in these pages includes family members, friends, and co-workers; but also butter, baseball, birds, and assorted articles of clothing.

Speaking of family members, this book is graced with the exceptional work of my favorite visual artist—and mother—Rose Marie Cunniffe. Rosie characterizes her art as "lyrical landscapes," which are mostly abstract paintings and often feature collage. My essay "Trouble-Making" (page 31) highlights similarities and differences in how we each approach a blank canvas or a blank page.

Rosie's creativity was apparent at an early age, but her true artistic journey began later in life. I was nearly fifty before I began to write my own true stories, but I knew it wasn't too late because I had watched my mother bloom as a visual artist in midlife. Our forms of self-expression are, at least on the surface, miles apart. We both tend toward the whimsical and the playful, but until we began to select the art for this book, from maybe forty years' worth of paintings, we both thought that was the only common thread that linked our art-making—and trouble-making—practices. We were happily surprised to find how many of the essays and images seemed to be made for each other, although the ink and the paint had long since dried before we considered our "pairings." We have cheered each other on at every stage of our artistic adventures. Now it is the pleasure of a lifetime to be published side by side.

The Journey, Day 1 • acrylic on board

Everything I Need to Know
I'm Still Learning from Mary Richards

> *"I'm an experienced woman. I've been around... Well, all right, I might not have been around, but I've been... nearby."*
>
> —Mary Richards

I WAS THE LAST TO LEAVE THE OFFICE THAT SEPTEMBER evening, after putting the final touches on a news release for the next day. Because I had a long commute and it was late, I picked up Chinese takeout on the way home. I let myself into my ground-floor apartment, switched on a lamp, and headed for the kitchen, where I dumped a box-shaped lump of rice and a pint of shrimp chow mein onto a plate. I'd made it home just in time to have dinner with an old friend—Mary Richards, the lead character on *The Mary Tyler Moore Show*. She was back on the airwaves in the early 1990s thanks to Nickelodeon's Nick at Nite, a line-up of nostalgic reruns aimed squarely at Baby Boomers like me.

Truth be told, my thirty-something self had been dining with Mary fairly often since I'd rediscovered her on cable television. I couldn't resist reliving those episodes from my teenage years. I laughed at the dated clothing and smiled at references to 1970s events and politics, thinking back on all the Saturday nights I'd spent with Mary and her friends. So while it wasn't at all unusual for me to be eating alone on a weeknight and watching a rerun of my favorite old show in my living room, it was quite a surprise when Nick at Nite served up that particular episode on that particular September evening, considering what I'd just done.

The episode opens with Mary hunched over a typewriter in her apartment where she's been working all weekend to update obituary files on famous people for WJM, the Minneapolis television news station where she works, in case some celebrity dies unexpectedly. Her best friend and neighbor, Rhoda, pops in, hoping to talk Mary into seeing a movie, but Mary insists she's got to keep working. So Rhoda joins her, and they make steady progress through the alphabet of celebrities until 4:00 am, when they are so tired and punchy—and still only up to the Ws—they start making things up, collapsing in fits of laughter with each new fake obituary. Silly stuff, like how Raquel Welch would not die by drowning. Finally, just before giving up, Rhoda and Mary craft an obituary for Wee Willie Williams, at 110 the oldest living citizen of Minneapolis, with a punchline about how when last interviewed he had "no immediate plans for the future, but hoped to include traveling, gardening, and breathing."

All of which struck me as highly amusing and weirdly coincidental, in view of my own role in crafting the aforementioned news release, which was not real news, but a prank for a coworker's fortieth birthday. A few of us had stayed late—until after our manager Steve went home—to inflate black balloons and scatter confetti across his desk and around the neat stacks of files that lined the windowsills of his corner office. The news release had been someone else's idea, but I had to agree it was a stroke of genius: a fake story on real press letterhead.

I kept thinking our fake news release was funny right up until the scene where Mary leaves the unfinished obituaries on her desk, unattended. Of course just before the evening news, word comes that Wee Willie has died, and of course anchorman Ted finds the fake copy and cluelessly reads it on the air. When their boss, Mr. Grant, realizes Mary is to blame, he's too angry to even talk to her that evening. He tells her to be in his office first thing the next morning.

Uh-oh.

During the commercial break, I started wondering if I should get in my car and make the fifty-mile round trip for the second time that day to undo what had seemed a few hours earlier like an innocent joke. Or should I just brace myself for a sleepless night and pray no one would inadvertently issue or take offense at what was obviously a fake news release, even though I'd gone to so much trouble to make it look authentic?

Back on my TV screen, on the morning after the fake obituary was read on the air, Mr. Grant marches into the newsroom looking like he's dressed for a funeral, in a black pin-striped suit, a white shirt, and a black tie. The formality and highly unusual unrumpledness of his clothes clearly establish the seriousness of the situation.

Mary is dressed mostly in white—a tailored suit with a knee-length skirt and a jacket cinched at the waist. She's wearing a caramel-colored turtleneck and matching pumps. She knows Mr. Grant is upset, but still she looks like a million bucks, certainly not like someone who's been awake all night worrying. The contrast of his black and her white suggests Mr. Grant is the bad guy here and Mary, as always, remains the good girl. Except this time, she isn't. She's crossed a line—unwittingly, and through circumstances that make perfect sense in a sitcom—but it's a line Mr. Grant cannot overlook.

"You can take any other liberty you want in any area. You can kid around all you want. But the news is sacred," he tells her. Mary has messed with the news. She has violated a code and, worst of all, made Mr. Grant's unwavering trust in her waver, if only temporarily.

"If this were anyone else...," Mr. Grant begins.

"Mr. Grant, I don't want any special treatment," Mary interrupts.

"Mary, this is the kind of thing they fire people for," he says, looking stricken.

"Mr. Grant, I'd appreciate any special treatment."

All of a sudden, my shrimp chow mein wasn't sitting so well. An innocent, news-related caper had landed my old friend Mary in hot water. She was going to be punished. Never mind that this was—and would continue to be—*The Mary Tyler Moore Show*, so of course the unpleasantness would have to be resolved in Mary's favor, and within the half hour. In real life, I wasn't so sure what might happen to me the next day.

Because here's what Mary Richards had not done: She had not papered the halls of her workplace with a news release with this headline: "Steve L. Turns 40, Looks Forward to Digital Rectal Exam." She had not taken a subject—early detection of prostate cancer—that her employer was in the forefront of promoting and turned it into the punchline for a joke.

In real time, my messing-with-the-news moment of synchronicity with Mary Richards happened during the era of

Murphy Brown, the hard-hitting, hard-living, potty-mouthed journalist portrayed so convincingly by Candice Bergen that then Vice President Dan Quayle picked a public fight with Brown about being a single mother—seemingly oblivious to the fact that she was a fictional character.

When forty-year-old Murphy first hit the airwaves in 1988, I was smitten. I was a thirty-year-old career woman who worked on the other side of the news—in the public relations department of a pharmaceutical company. In fact, on the very day in 1992 when Dan Quayle famously misspelled "potatoe" in an elementary school, his wife Marilyn visited my company to promote breast cancer screening. (Guess which story made national news?) I admired Murphy's intelligence, her confidence, her sense of humor, her willingness to challenge authority and break rules in the service of truthful reporting. I was inclined to agree with her politics, though not too publicly around the office, where Murphy's left-leaning views were highly unpopular.

I *liked* Murphy Brown, but I wasn't *like* her. And even though occasionally I might have wished I could channel her bravado, I knew I would never become a Murphy kind of a woman. I was, and always had been, far more like Mary Richards, the not-so-hard-hitting, mostly clean-living, well-mannered television news producer portrayed by Mary Tyler Moore.

In more ways than one, I'd grown up with Mary Richards, who landed that job at WJM when she was 30 and I was nearly 12. Mary and the gang at WJM—Lou, the crusty but soft-hearted curmudgeon; Ted, the buffoonish baritone; quick-witted, self-effacing Murray; and self-assured, vampy Sue Ann—kept me entertained throughout my formative years, often on nights when I had babysitting gigs and had to be sure to put the kids to bed before Mary came on.

I loved that Mary lived in her own apartment in a city she'd moved to by herself; back then I lived with my parents, six younger siblings, and my grandfather in suburbia. I loved that big "M" sculpture on her wall; up to that point, a glued-together 1,000-piece puzzle was my boldest interior design statement. I loved straight-shooting, hippie-ish Rhoda, especially when she took on their wacky friend and landlord Phyllis. And oh, how I loved Mary's clothes; her taste informed my fashion decisions, or more accurately, my fashion fantasies. I still recall a plaid pantsuit with a cropped jacket and bell-bottom pants I wore in high school, thinking it was "very Mary."

At first, *The Mary Tyler Moore Show* was just good entertainment. It took a few seasons before I began to understand that what was going on went far deeper than stories about producing the evening news or making friends in a new city. Mary Richards offered a distinctly different view of how a "modern" woman might find her way in the world, particularly the world of work. Through Mary, I began to absorb lessons about how things were changing for women, the choices that were available, and the consequences of choosing (or being chosen by) a non-traditional path—like that of a single career woman. I was too young to appreciate that this was ground-breaking territory for a television sitcom, but I knew Mary was different from most of the adult women in my world, almost all of whom were married or widowed. In that world, if a woman wasn't married, or hadn't been, she was trying to be. The only other alternatives I could see were to enter the convent or be written off as an "old maid." So I was interested in watching Mary's story unfold, even if I didn't expect my story would end up being like hers.

Mary's run at WJM lasted into my second semester of college. I watched the final episode in March 1977 with my closest girlfriends. We laughed, we cried, we staged our own little group hug as the cast shuffled out of the newsroom for the last time, incongruously singing "It's a Long Way to Tipperary." I had just learned in a literature class that comic endings are always contrived, and I felt rather clever for connecting that thought with the series finale.

The idea of Mary Richards stayed with me long after the final credits rolled. I can't say I consciously invoked her memory during my early years as a working girl. If I thought of her at all, it was fondly. But if I thought about my future, I was certain it would include a husband and children. I never expected to be an independent career woman like Mary. I never tried to model my life on hers.

Yet by the early 1990s, while I alternated between new episodes of *Murphy Brown* and reruns of *The Mary Tyler Moore Show*, my life was looking more like Mary's all the time. I had my own apartment, a genuine career, friendly neighbors, and occasional blind dates that were at least as bad as any of Mary's (okay, worse, because they were real). I even had a big metal "E" on my wall, a gift from a friend who had no way of knowing my history with Mary.

In fact, although I didn't figure this out until much later, on that September evening when I messed with the news and then watched episode twenty from season four—"Better Late... That's a Pun... Than Never"—I had caught up to Mary Richards in age. I was on the brink of turning thirty-four, the age she would forever be in reruns from that season. And like Mary, I was unaccustomed to getting myself into disciplinary trouble at work.

In college, I briefly flirted with trouble at my part-time job at the information desk at Philadelphia International Airport. Without cell phones, the internet, or monitors with flight times, our staff provided vital services, looking up flight schedules, giving out phone numbers for hotels and shuttles, and calling the airport operator to have people paged. On evenings and weekends, the desk was left in the hands of students like me and my friend Tina. If the phone wasn't ringing and we'd finished our homework, we had to find other ways to pass the time.

Maybe it was my idea, but I'm sure it was Tina who phoned in the page, at least the first time. Soon, the guys at the airline counter across from our desk were onto us, but the switchboard operators never caught on. Time after time, all through the halls of the airport, they'd broadcast our request: "Mr. Right, please come to the information desk in Terminal C. Mr. Right, to the information desk in Terminal C." We wanted to ask them to page "the (W)Right Brothers," so there'd be one for each of us, but as funny as that would have been in an airport, we knew it would end our little game, which we played sparingly, but to our own great amusement, for months.

That is, until the night when a middle-aged man, weighted down by a garment bag slung over one shoulder and a suitcase in the other hand, huffed and puffed his way to our desk, introducing himself as "Mr. Right" and apologizing for how long it had taken to reach us, but he'd been two terminals away when he heard the page.

Uh-oh. Tina and I looked at each other nervously, and her wide brown eyes made it clear it was up to me, being two years older, to find a way out of this situation.

"What's your first name?" I politely stammered.

"Thomas," he replied, still catching his breath.

"Oh, I'm sorry, we were looking for Mr. *William* Right," I said, disappointedly.

"That's OK, thanks anyway," he replied, hoisting his luggage and staggering back in the direction from which he'd come. Once he was out of earshot, we collapsed into laughter, tinged with leftover panic.

After that, Tina and I were done with fake pages. We would have gotten a good talking-to from our boss if we'd been found out, but since we were college kids (and two of his favorites), I doubt there would have been serious disciplinary action. Still, up until the night of the fake news release, paging Mr. Right was the riskiest thing I'd ever done at work.

In the fake obituary episode, Mary leaves Mr. Grant's office with a two-week suspension without pay. With Murray's encouragement, she marches back in and says she'd rather be fired than suspended. Lou lets her decide, and since she has backed herself into a principled corner, Mary gathers her sparse personal effects—box of tissues, spare pantyhose, hairspray, umbrella, and her signature bud vase—and leaves WJM in a daze.

In my 1990s living room, I paced and wrung my hands, trying to decide which was worse: calling attention to the fake news release if a security guard found me at work so late; or leaving the evidence in plain sight until the next morning. I reminded myself I didn't even write the worst bits of the release; a coworker had written most of it, including that tasteless headline. Still, I was the one to finish it, the one who made copies, left fingerprints all over the crime scene. Crime scene? Was it that bad? Could they actually trace the document to me? Were my fingerprints at the copy machine, on the stapler? How clever my coworker had been, inventing a reason to leave earlier, forwarding the draft to me so it would be saved on my computer. He'd probably already deleted it from his.

In the end, of course, Mary goes back to work at WJM. After half-heartedly looking for employment elsewhere, she begs Mr. Grant to give her back her old job: "I wanna come back," she says through sobs. "I don't like it out there." He happily rehires her, confident she has learned her lesson.

In real life, I didn't go back to work on that September night, but I sure didn't get much sleep. Every time I closed my eyes, Mr. Grant appeared, sternly telling Mary (and me), "You have to be punished." But as it turned out, the fake news release was a big hit in my office. In fact, my good-girl reputation slipped half a notch when word got around that I was one of the perpetrators.

Still, like Mary, I had learned my lesson. I never messed with the news again.

I kept watching those reruns in the 1990s until Mary and the gang came full circle, back to their now-famous group hug. With Monday-through-Friday episodes, they sped through the 1970s in a time-warping way, even as they stayed stuck in the past. When the reruns stopped, I appreciated the show far more than I had as a teenager. I knew by then how hard a woman still had to work to be taken seriously, more than twenty years after Mary had proven herself. I understood just how elusive Mr. Right could be, especially when a woman spent so much of her time in the office or in airports, crisscrossing the country and even the Atlantic Ocean on business trips. And maybe I read a little too much into one small gesture from the opening credits, where Mary shrugs as she tosses a package of meat into her shopping cart; but by the 1990s every time that image flashed on my television screen, I felt certain I could describe the full range of emotions Mary was feeling in that moment: "Yes, dinner for one, again." "What the heck, I deserve a nice steak once in a while." "Who cares what the cashier thinks?" Sometimes I caught myself making that same gesture and thinking those same thoughts while wandering through a grocery store.

Mostly, I think, at the end of my second go-round with *The Mary Tyler Moore Show*, what I loved best was Mary's resilience, her unflappable optimism, how week after week, regardless of how things had gone at work or with her latest romance, she still tossed her tasseled hat high into the chilly Minneapolis air and started all over again. Sometimes I found myself consciously channeling that feeling, on good days as well as bad.

I knew I would always have that moment—my very-Mary moment—of nearly losing my job (well, not really) over a prank that backfired on precisely the same night when episode twenty from season four just happened to air on Nick at Nite. Now when I thought about Mary—and over the next years I still did from time to time—I would feel a little closer to her. I could see how my story was beginning to look more and more like hers, as I reached my late thirties, still single, still a hard-working career girl who'd somehow gone off script from the life she'd expected. Mary's story provided a point of reference as I navigated through that stage of my life.

The year I turned forty, *Entertainment Weekly* named *The Mary Tyler Moore Show* the best TV show of all time, which made me quite happy. Two years later, ABC (not CBS, the show's old network) aired a two-hour telemovie that reunited Mary and Rhoda in New York City, a quarter-century after they'd parted in Minneapolis. The original idea had been a series featuring middle-aged Mary and Rhoda, but the network decided to test it with a movie pilot. I couldn't wait. Finally, I would know how life had turned out for Mary. (Of course, I understood Mary was a fictional character. I wasn't Dan Quayle, after all, I could tell the difference. But still . . .)

Sometimes I wish I hadn't watched that movie. Ten minutes in, I knew it was a mistake—watching it, definitely, and making it, probably. Perhaps because the movie had flashed forward all those years, and we didn't *see* Mary finally meeting and marrying Mr. Right—a congressman, recently deceased when the movie begins—and becoming a wife and a mother, for me it just didn't ring true. Maybe she seemed out of place in New York, or as a widow. Or maybe—just maybe—it was because watching that movie made me realize that part of the appeal of the way *The Mary Tyler Moore Show* ended was that I could always imagine—but never know—how Mary's life had turned out. And as long as I didn't know, I suppose I always imagined—or wanted to—that she was still out there somewhere, making it on her own, making it after all, as an independent, unmarried woman. Like me.

I wasn't the only one who didn't like *Mary and Rhoda*. The series was canceled before it ever began, and critics panned the movie. One review in the *San Francisco Chronicle* said: "*Mary and Rhoda* is to be savored, ever so briefly, for its reunion of Mary Richards and Rhoda Morgenstern. And then it should be spat out like sour milk, in hopes of preserving the happier memory of Mary and Rhoda in their 1970s sitcom heaven."

I did my best to forget the movie. I preferred to remember the thirty-seven-year-old Mary who lost her job when a new station manager took over at WJM, leaving her story unfinished. When faced with a challenging workplace or relationship situation, I sometimes found myself wondering, "What would Mary do?"

When at the age of forty-two I bought my first house, then had to carry myself across the threshold—on crutches, with a broken ankle and a knee-high cast—it occurred to me that my first day as a homeowner would have made a great episode of *The Mary Tyler Moore Show*. (Mary, of course, would have been surrounded by friends in that episode, whereas I was lucky enough to have an army of family members to help me move in while I waved my crutches around to show them what went where.)

In 2005, I bumped into Mary once more, in reruns on some random cable station. I'd just left that pharmaceutical company where I'd worked for nearly two decades, and I was spending a lot of time thinking about what the next phase of my career might look like. So I tuned in again, looking for whatever wisdom Mary might have to offer. I started paying closer attention to the episodes. I noticed little things, like the wicker trunk in Mary's first apartment that she used as a coffee table; I'd had one just like it in my first apartment, but I could no longer recall if I'd consciously copied Mary's decor or if that had been a coincidence. I noticed that the suit Lou wore when he punished Mary in season four—the one that made him look like he was dressed for a funeral—was the very suit he did wear in season five to the funeral for Chuckles the Clown, an episode that still is considered an all-time sitcom classic, nearly five decades later.

The third time around, I noticed bigger things, too, like how Mary's singleness sometimes set her apart from the people around her, but also how she never let it define her, at least not completely. Also, I liked that she was a quiet kind of a feminist, compared with, say, Phyllis, who looked for slights and fights everywhere; Mary earned respect as a woman in a mostly male world, but she never demanded respect just because she was a woman.

I started searching online for information about the show. I ordered season four on DVDs, so I could watch episode twenty again. I watched other episodes too. I had forgotten that Mary had taken a creative writing class, something I'd just done myself after a quarter-century of writing words for other people but never for me. I squirmed through the episode where Mary and Rhoda have a falling out ("Best of Enemies"), although I loved this bit of dialogue:

>Rhoda: "Boy, Mary, you know something? You've got a real *Ms.* job."
>Mary: "What do you mean?
>Rhoda: "This is the kind of job Gloria Steinem wants you to have."

I recalled times during my own career when female friends had made similar comments to me. Not that they would have mentioned Gloria Steinem or *Ms.* magazine, just that they seemed to think my jobs were more glamorous or more prestigious than they'd felt to me, mostly because I did so much traveling. Once my old airport friend Tina, whom I'd lost track of years earlier, saw my name in the newspaper when I got a promotion and phoned to say hello; turns out she'd actually met her Mr. Right while still working at the airport, and now they were married and had a young family. Tina asked about my work, and I suppose I made it sound exciting—that seemed to be what she was hoping for. But really, like Mary, at that point I'd spent much of my career making men around me look good, while I only advanced a rung or two up the ladder. I'd been a medical writer and editor, a public relations and communications professional, I'd cranked out more academic papers, news releases, newsletters, and speeches for doctors and executives than I could count. A couple of times I'd turned down opportunities to move a rung or two further up the ladder into jobs I didn't want, even if they had bigger titles. I'm pretty sure Gloria Steinem wouldn't have been impressed.

In 2006, between jobs, I finally started writing about me and Mary—the earliest draft of an essay about the night of the fake news release—but I didn't get far. Other stories I wanted to tell seemed more pressing. Always, though, I knew Mary was there—in my notes, in my mind, in those DVDs collecting dust on a bookshelf. I always knew I'd find my way back to her and thank her for all she'd taught me over the years about being a single career woman.

A few years later, I ran into Steve—he of the fortieth birthday and the fake news release—and he mentioned he still had a copy of that old relic somewhere, and it still makes him laugh every time he happens upon it. Which got me thinking about me and Mary all over again.

I went back to season four and mined those episodes for all they were worth. I still wanted more, so I ordered up season seven, the final season, which is loaded with emotional truths about being a single working woman—some triumphant, some disappointing, some both at the same time. Like Mary having—at last—the authority to select a new sportscaster for WJM and making the bold choice to hire a woman, then having to fire her because she did such a lousy job. I also found yet another episode about Mary trying to find her voice as a creative writer, a thread I'd missed before.

Then I discovered *Mary and Lou and Rhoda and Ted (And All the Brilliant Minds Who Made The Mary Tyler Moore Show a Classic)*, a 2013 book by Jennifer Keishin Armstrong. I'd already come to appreciate what a ground-breaking move it had been to present a thirty-year-old, unmarried woman as the lead character in a television sitcom back in 1970. What I hadn't appreciated until I read the book was how many women—in addition to the actors who played Mary and Rhoda, Sue Ann and Georgette, Phyllis and her daughter Beth—had contributed to that trail-blazing production, which lasted for 168 episodes. Women writers, in particular, who'd had trouble finding steady television or movie work, for the first time were sought after and valued for their abilities to tell true—or seemingly so—stories about themselves, their friends, their mothers, their daughters, their work, their changing world; and all through Mary Richards. Trail-blazing women who made it possible for a female reporter like Murphy Brown to hit the airwaves a generation later. It seems likely that if Mary hadn't paved the way, Murphy might never have seen the light of day.

Mary Tyler Moore, according to Armstrong, "tried—but failed—to play down talk of being a 'symbol' to women." I'll vouch for how thoroughly she failed—and not just for myself—because every fifty- or sixty-something woman I mention Mary Richards to agrees that her story mattered, that it resonated, that she seemed so real (except for those oh-so-fake 1970s eyelashes) that it's hard to think of her as a fictional character. Armstrong also says of Moore, "She just wanted to be remembered as someone who always looked for the truth. Even, as she once said, if it wasn't funny."

And sometimes it wasn't. Mary Richards struggled mightily to be taken seriously, to trust her own instincts, to stand up for her beliefs. She wrestled with diversity in the workplace and glass ceilings long before anyone used those terms. She had to learn to work with difficult people, and sometimes she had to live with other people getting—or taking—credit for her efforts. And no matter how hard she tried to downplay her chronic state of singleness, someone always seemed to be asking, often out loud, why a nice girl like Mary couldn't find a man.

Which brings me back to the final season and that concept of comic endings always being contrived. In drama, a "comic" (or happy) story generally ends with a celebration, often a wedding banquet. The cast and producers of *The Mary Tyler Moore Show* knew before season seven began that it would be their last. They teased their audience with Mary's story ending on a happily-ever-after romantic note. In one episode, she dates a charming sixty-something man. In another, we see through imagined scenes what her life might have been like if she'd married Murray, Ted, or Lou. And in the penultimate episode, Mary asks Lou for a date, a date that's a comically wonderful failure. It becomes obvious to all that Mary Richards will end as she began, as a single working woman, albeit older and wiser, with far more confidence than she had in season one. No Mr. Right, no wedding banquet, still making it on her own, but not unhappily so.

Still—and again, I *do* know Mary Richards was a fictional character, not a real person—I sometimes wish I could see her now. Not as she was in that telemovie, but as she might be if she had stayed single and kept working. I want to meet her for a drink or, better yet, take her out for shrimp chow mein and catch up on all the years since 1977—hers and mine. We'd hit it off, I just know we would. I'd want to hear how she reinvented herself after she left WJM; did she stay in journalism or try something new? I'd want to tell her about the bumps in my own career, and the big shift I made in my forties, away from the corporate world (happily) and into the nonprofit sector. I'd ask if she ever did find her voice as a writer. I hope she did because I'd love to compare notes on what that was like for each of us. I'd want to know if she ever worked for a woman boss and if she too sometimes found that surprisingly harder than working for a man. I'll bet we could have fun comparing Mr. Grant with—just as one example—a demanding and self-aggrandizing boss who didn't grasp how a shared online calendar worked and had to be told everyone in the company could see she was scheduled for a Brazilian wax. I'd want to know if, like me, Mary found a few trusty single women friends to travel with, to have adventures with, to cook for, to see movies with, to talk with about our chronic state of singlehood—and its flip side, our chronic state of independence. I'd have to ask how she got by with no brothers or sisters, no in-laws or nieces or nephews; I can't imagine being single *and* being an only child.

I have a funny feeling that, like me, Mary would eventually have stopped going on blind dates, maybe because people stopped offering to fix her up or maybe because the offers just kept getting worse. I'm pretty sure she, like me, would have steered clear entirely of online dating sites, concluding that there are worse ways to live than being single. And, I might add, far worse ways to see yourself than as someone whose life—at least some of the time—might lend itself to a situation comedy.

I know the curtain had to be brought down on Mary Richards; no sitcom lasts forever. And so it was, way back in 1977, with Mary, Lou, Murray, and Sue Ann all being fired in the final episode while Ted, miraculously, comically, keeps his job at WJM. The cast leaves the newsroom for the final time. Mary leans back in through the door, alone, to flick off the light, and then she disappears into an unscripted future. Which is, at least for me, where she will always remain. It is, as they say, a long way to Tipperary.

Trouble-Making

These troubles are all self-inflicted, all clearly traceable to the moment when one of us picked up a paintbrush or a pen and decided to make some art.

I WAS STUCK. I'D WRITTEN MYSELF INTO A CORNER AND couldn't seem to find my way back out. The trouble, on that occasion, was one of structure. A piece of narrative nonfiction I'd been working on for ages had at last begun to take shape. But in the process of developing my story, I'd wandered off in a new direction—one I happened to like—then found myself struggling to build a bridge back to the point where I'd taken my detour.

While I was staring at the page on my computer screen (as if that had ever solved anything) the phone rang. My mother, checking on a Saturday afternoon to see what I was up to.

"I'm trying to fix a problem with an essay I am working on," I told her.

"Oh, that happens to me too," she said. "It's funny when you think about it. As artists we create our own problems, then we don't know how to fix them. There isn't a problem there until you start working on a project, then before you know it you've made all kinds of trouble for yourself."

I'd never thought of it that way before.

The problems Mom creates are different from mine. She's a visual artist, and her works are almost always abstract paintings. I'm a writer, and my works are almost always creative nonfiction. So in many ways we live at opposite ends of the storytelling spectrum. Except that we both always start with some variation of the blank page. And perhaps a vague idea of what we're trying to say, although I think we'd both agree that at the outset, there's a lot of experimentation involved, even when you think you know what it is you want to make sense of, or document, or just express.

The pleasure—and often the trouble—begins once you've made a first pass at the work, and then you begin "finding" things you didn't know were there. The essay or the prose poem lures you down a path you hadn't meant to follow. The painting or collage asks you to mind what's going on in the lower left corner or underneath that fragment from another piece that you just affixed to the canvas.

I suspect our troubles—mine and Mom's—are more alike than our art forms. Troubles with composition and balance. Troubles with juxtaposition—whether in time or in space. Troubles with scale, with tone, with an overabundance of material. Troubles with revision—deleting, painting over, cutting and pasting; or tugging a bit too hard on one thread in the work and watching the whole piece unravel. These troubles are all self-inflicted, all clearly traceable to the moment when one of us picked up a paintbrush or a pen and decided to make some art.

And then there's the trouble of naming the work, which we writers can't help but do, or at least most of us, most of the time. Poets sometimes get away with "untitled," while visual artists do it all the time. I don't get that. I think every piece of artwork deserves a title. I won't buy a piece of visual art if the artist didn't go to the trouble of naming it.

Whenever Mom shows me one of her new paintings, I have a habit of asking, "What is it called?"

She has grown weary of responding, "Why does that matter?"

And so more often than not she has a title ready when I ask; a few times I'm pretty sure she's made them up on the spot just to humor me. I'm only looking for a hint, a way into her abstract pieces. And she always does give them names, at least before she sends them out in public. Good names, too, often whimsical or even inquisitive.

But she doesn't like to tell me the names, at least not right away. She'd rather I find my own meanings in her work, and often I do, pointing out shapes or other elements she hasn't put there on purpose. Maybe I insist on a title because I'm a writer, and I make sense of things through words. But I'm also curious to know what she was thinking about, or experimenting with, when she picked up her paintbrush; or perhaps more importantly, after she put it down, satisfied that her work was done.

If it ever is done. Because we both agree, even after we've sent our work out into the world, almost always there are changes we'd like to make to something that's now frozen in print/cyberspace or hanging on someone else's living room wall. Trouble we've made, problems we'd like to fix.

Trouble is, once it's out there, it's out there. Even if we're the only ones who can see the flaws or, more kindly, how much better the next iteration would have been.

Mom knows my rule about not buying untitled art. But one day quite by chance we landed on a phrase that might make me bend that rule. Another call from her to see what I was up to—this one to my office, not my home. Instead of the usual "private caller" flashing on the screen when my phone rang, it said "name withheld." We laughed about that, and I told her if I ever saw a painting with that label, I might be tempted to take it home. I'd like knowing that it had a name. I'd like living with the mystery of not knowing what that name was. And I couldn't help wondering—every time I looked at the piece—what kind of trouble the artist hoped to avoid by keeping that name to herself.

Wonderland • acrylic on paper

Sibling Revelry

> *Dad has succeeded in calming us down and getting us worked up at the same time. He's gotten us thinking and playing and dreaming along with each other, head to head, toe to toe, right there under the Christmas tree.*

I AM TRYING TO FIND A WAY INTO THIS STORY, ONE THAT will help you understand The Project, and by extension the man behind The Project, namely, my dad.

This isn't easy, because the story has a lot of moving parts; it spans several decades, and it has a ridiculous number of characters, none of whom can be given short shrift because this is an ensemble piece, and each member of the cast carries as much weight as the next.

I've gone around in circles trying to find an opening, a window into the proceedings. All roads lead back to the family Christmas tree at 441 Highland Terrace, my childhood home from the age of five and the only place I ever remember spending Christmas day until quite recently. I'm dialing all the way back to a time when our tree was adorned with hand-painted-and-glittered walnut-shell ornaments, then dusted with fake plastic snowflakes, which we also liberally sprinkled on each other, accidentally on purpose of course.

Let's call it 1967, although any Christmas Eve in the mid-1960s will do, the only difference being how many of us are still wearing fuzzy, footsie pajamas.

Dad has finally wrestled a sweet-smelling, slightly lopsided Christmas tree into place and untangled the string of lights with fragile, tube-shaped bulbs, already in their second decade of service. He's managed to drape them around the tree evenly enough to secure Mom's approval. I've helped a bit, being the oldest, but I'm only nine, and I can't reach too high, so mostly I've just unpuddled the lights from the floor and handed them up to Dad, who's using a kitchen chair as a stepladder.

Mom is in the kitchen, cleaning up from dinner, thinking of all the elfish work still to be done before she can call it a day: supervise the rest of the tree-decorating and stocking-hanging, then bundle the five of us off to bed. (On Christmas Eve in 1967 there are still only five siblings, although we know twin babies are expected in the spring, right around Easter.)

After we're nestled snug in our beds, Mom will still have to fill the stockings with care; wrap, label, and stack what must seem like (and could well be) a hundred presents, including a few for her and Dad, and a few more for our housemates, Mom's father, our Pop-Pop, and her brother, our Uncle Mickey. So she's savoring this patch of relative peace in the kitchen, knowing Dad has the next little while sewn up in the playroom.

Those of us old enough to remember our Christmas Eve tradition can hardly contain ourselves. We don't want to spoil it for the little guys. (Pete is only three.) But we want them to know it's going to be *so great*. Angie and I may be jumping up and down in anticipation. There might be just the teensiest bit of jockeying for position between Brian and Dennis when they can tell Dad is almost ready to begin.

With one look he settles us, and in a flash we're all flat on our backs, feet under the lowest branches of the tree, faces pointed toward the ceiling, one big gap more or less in the middle where Dad will squeeze in among us. Then Dad turns off the overhead light. He crawls to the outlet on the wood-paneled wall near the back of the tree.

"Is everyone ready?" he asks.

"Yes," we cry out in one voice. "Plug it in!"

And there on the playroom ceiling a whole new world opens up—a land of shadows, projected through the branches of the tree, tinted by the red and blue and green and yellow bulbs. Dad wriggles in among us and points to a spot just to the left of the treetop. "Up there," he says, "is a road that leads into the forest. I see a group of boys and girls walking along that road. I wonder where they might be going."

That one tiny suggestion is all it takes to set our storytelling in motion.

We point, we gesture, we invent.

We laugh, we gasp, we sigh.

We find rivers, roads, and birds in the shadows, then bad guys, and good guys, and angels. We're sure we can make out a team of flying reindeer and a jolly fellow in a red and white suit driving a toy-stuffed sled. We interrupt each other—but not too aggressively, this being Christmas Eve and all of us being on our best behavior. Our story twists and turns across the ceiling as we try to impress Dad—and outdo each other—with improbable plot detours, magical discoveries, and strange sound effects. By now Mom is hovering in the doorway, enjoying Dad's annual ritual. We stay there on the floor for as long as we're allowed, until it's time to finish trimming the tree and then hang up our stockings.

Dad has succeeded in calming us down and getting us worked up at the same time. He's gotten us thinking and playing and dreaming along with each other, head to head, toe to toe, right there under the Christmas tree.

Now, fast forward to Christmas Day, 1990.

We're too big to squeeze in under the tree, and a little old for the game with the Christmas lights, even though not one Christmas passes without somebody recalling that old tradition. By now there are several more of us: Angie, Brian, Dennis, and Pete are all married, and Dennis has two little daughters. We don't know it yet, but by spring there will be two new babies born in another part of the world who will be joining Angie's family as adopted siblings before next Christmas.

Some of us spent Christmas Eve in our own houses or apartments, maybe with in-laws. But we've all managed to come home for Christmas dinner, and this is one of the last years we'll all be able to organize ourselves to be here like this, geographically speaking.

The presents have all been unwrapped, the stockings emptied. Now with grandchildren in the mix, the number of presents has increased exponentially.

We've just about cleared up all the paper and bows and bags

when Dad waltzes into the living room with a big brown cardboard box. Mom has come in from the kitchen to watch. With great ceremony, Dad presents each of the seven siblings with identical unpainted wooden birdhouses, which he has constructed himself over the last few months while recovering from a heart attack (his first, but not only).

He instructs us to paint or otherwise finish his handcrafted objects, turn them in to him by early March, and be prepared to let the guests at Angie and Rich's St. Patty's Day party vote on who has delivered the best "project."

And just like that, Dad has turned us into kids again. He's gathered us around the tree at what we now call "Club 441," he's figuratively plugged in the lights and given us the beginning of a new story, and now it's "game on." He's gotten us thinking and playing and dreaming along with each other once again, right there in the shadow of another Christmas tree.

We're already imagining all the ways we might impress him—and outdo each other—when March rolls around. It's safe to assume there will be improbable plot detours, magical discoveries, strange sound effects, and as always, lots and lots of laughter.

I know, I know. According to Tolstoy, "All happy families are alike; each unhappy family is unhappy in its own way." Not that any family is happy all the time, and I suspect even the unhappy ones have occasional moments of joy. But somehow that opening line from *Anna Karenina* has been twisted into an unwritten rule against writing about happy families. Mr. Tolstoy, I beg to differ, but you haven't met my family, and I've never met anyone else with a family tradition quite like ours.

So fast forward one more time, to March 2014, as we teeter on the brink of a quarter-century of playing along with The Project, telling our stories year after year after year. Only now, in hindsight, does it occur to me that our first project, Dad's handcrafted birdhouses, might have been a not-so-subtle reference to my parents' rapidly emptying nest.

Really, though, I think Dad was just trying to mess with us. He'd figured out a new way to tap into our creativity, while he stepped back and waited to see what we'd do with his unfinished carpentry work.

Anyway, the birdhouse competition was a big hit at the 1991 St.

Patty's Day party. So the next year he gave us bits of wooden scraps and dowels, and the next year we got children's playing blocks, and the next year it was popsicle sticks. Echoes of childhood, placed into the hands of adult siblings, each time challenging us—and our respective and often-expanding households—to turn them into individual creations, while simultaneously turning us loose on each other as fiercely friendly competitors.

Over the years the raw materials we've received have sometimes been sentimental (family photos), sometimes seemingly random (bags of clear marbles), other times just plain weird (cans of SPAM). The projects we've delivered have included well-made pieces of furniture, working robotics, musical performances, short films, essays, appetizers, poems, puppets, and elaborate costumes.

Often our assignments are delivered in plain #10 envelopes with the words "Project Control" typed in the top left-hand corner. Sometimes the letters are business-like, other times they are philosophical, reflective, or nostalgic.

Sometimes the rules are incredibly specific: "You have each received a total of 450 craft sticks. You must use at least 425 of them." Other years they are deliberately vague: "Make a contemporary work of art out of the materials I have provided." (Those materials included circuit boards from old computers, which had fallen into Dad's hands through volunteer work at our old high school.)

"My Dear Boys and Girls," the earliest letters began, although many of us were well into adulthood. I was 32 when we got our birdhouses, and the twins, Amy and Jen, were 22.

Over time "My Dear Daughters and Sons" has been the most common salutation, although Dad tries to be inclusive; for example, he's gone with "My Dear Daughters and Sons (Outlaws included)," using the nickname my sisters- and brothers-in-law gave themselves years ago. But he likes to mix it up. Once he referenced our birth order with "My Dear Daughters (2), Sons (3), and More Daughters (2)"; once he went with "My Dear Sons and Daughters (used to be Boys and Girls)." And over time he has tipped his hat to the second—and now *third*—generation of Projecteers, addressing one letter to "Ladies and Gentlemen . . . Boys and Girls of All Ages."

In addition to being the most inclusive salutation in Dad's repertoire, that last one best establishes his role as ringmaster in the family circus he orchestrates every spring as we enthusiastically present our projects to be judged, and The Project to be celebrated.

The project letters have been signed by "Dad," "Santa Claus (the real one)," "Project Control" and (since the arrival of grandchildren) "Pop."

As if we didn't know.

Stitches in Nine

Together, we stare at the radio, our hopes pinned to that distant diamond. Sometimes we talk back to it, in disbelief or in joy.

I've commandeered the dining room table, unfurled the cutting mat, lined up my tools. The sewing machine sits at the head of the table, its hot, bright bulb illuminating my immediate work space. My left hand feeds layers of fabric slowly under the presser foot, while my right hand extracts each pin before it reaches the needle. Within arm's reach—but not too close to the pattern-shaped pieces of fabric I've cut out and pinned together—is a glass of iced tea, covered with beads of sweat.

In the next room, my grandfather has commandeered the far end of the kitchen table, the evening paper held high, at arm's length. He is simultaneously working his way through the day's news and through a bowl of orange Jell-O floating in milk, a concoction I'll never comprehend, though for years my sister and I have faithfully taken turns dissolving that sugary powder in boiling water to keep him ever-supplied with his favorite treat.

On the kitchen desk sits a clunky black radio. And though we each have our own reasons for wanting to be awake at this late hour while the rest of the household slumbers; and though we make no effort to converse as I stitch and sip and he reads and slurps; and though there never will be more than a tacit acknowledgment that we are each glad to have the other nearby, we know we are in this thing together. We are listening to a staticky late-night broadcast of a Phillies game from the West Coast in the distant 1970s when most of our baseball experiences were transmitted through that radio.

I've learned to calibrate my pressure on the foot pedal to the cadences of the play-by-play, slowing down or finding other tasks when the game gets interesting, speeding up during commercials or when things start going south for the Phils. The radio has to be low enough not to disturb my slumbering parents and six siblings, but loud enough to carry into the dining room over a chorus of crickets and the attic exhaust fan.

We take turns adjusting the antenna or fiddling with the dial when the signal starts to fade, which it does pretty often, especially during summer storms, and almost always at critical moments. When Mike Schmidt laces one over the fence or Steve Carlton notches another strikeout, I lean forward in my chair, grinning, and he lets his newspaper dip to catch my eye. Occasionally, a situation on the Astroturf three thousand miles away is so promising or so dire that I temporarily abandon my station and join him in the kitchen, and he lays down his paper. Together, we stare at the radio, our hopes pinned to that distant diamond. Sometimes we talk back to it, in disbelief or in joy.

But mostly we are silent partners, sharing the relative quiet of a summer night, the rustle of turning pages, the steady stitches from my Kenmore, and the well-known yet never-predictable rhythms of a game we both love. A game with enough pregnant pauses to accommodate my efforts to stitch together new clothes for the fall. A game with enough narrative threads to hold our interest well past midnight. We rely equally on the announcers and the sounds of the game—ball on leather, ball on wood, umpire's voice, cheers or moans from the crowd—to "see" each play unfold.

In my memory, this is a long-running ritual—my grandfather, me, my sewing machine, the radio. In real life, I realize, it played out over just a season or two—my first summers after high school, his last summers to enjoy baseball. Seasons leading up to the Phillies' first World Series championship in 1980, which he didn't live to see. Maybe we shared a dozen late-night games this way, maybe not even that many. But enough to leave a pattern.

I still love baseball on the radio, although these days I'm more likely to listen in my car than in my house. I almost never use my sewing machine anymore—that same one, which I've had for more than forty years. But in my mind, baseball on the radio has a background soundtrack that includes the revving of a sewing machine motor. And on those rare occasions when I hem a new set of curtains, even in the depths of winter, I could swear I hear the ghost of a game of baseball as I measure, trace, pin, and stitch.

Hoop-de-do • acrylic on canvas

Necessary Things

> *My earliest memory of the bear is seeing it tucked away in my mother's cedar chest for safekeeping. Because she saved it, I came to know it as a treasure.*

Gray Bunny

BEFORE GRACE NAMES IT, THE SMALL STUFFED BUNNY IS pale pink with purple dots and wears a lavender bow around his neck. A cherished playmate for my littlest niece, he is clutched close at bedtime and in the car seat. Eventually she learns to introduce him, dangling him by an ear and announcing "Bunny," giggling at her own ability to speak.

With so much affection and milk lavished on him, the bunny makes regular trips through the washing machine. Soon the pink fur fades and the original ribbon frays and then falls off, only to be replaced with a rapid succession of other-colored ribbons, as Grace gets better and better at undoing the knots.

Meanwhile Grace's vocabulary grows, as does her collection of inanimate friends. She names them all, but the one she loves best is the one she calls "Gray Bunny." By now he truly is gray, with only the palest of dots flecking his thinning fur.

Everyone in Grace's world learns to take note of Gray Bunny's whereabouts. In addition to Mommy and Daddy, her grandparents, aunts, uncles, cousins, and neighborhood babysitters all learn to do Gray Bunny checks on a regular basis. Gray Bunny has to be in the car, beside the pillow, close to the bathtub, or near the kitchen table. On the day Grace meets her baby brother, Gray Bunny goes along for moral support. Once when she visits cousins in another state, Gray Bunny inadvertently stays home, making bedtime nearly unbearable for the entire household.

Sometimes Grace goes for an hour without mentioning Gray Bunny. Then she remembers, and her need is urgent. Whenever he re-appears, Grace greets him with "Oh, *there* you are," as if they'd been playing hide-and-seek.

Life without Gray Bunny is unimaginable, or so we all think, until he goes missing for good, left behind who-knows-where on an otherwise ordinary day. Grace's mommy phones every place they have been on that day, but Gray Bunny is nowhere to be found. Grace is heartbroken at first, although once the initial shock wears off, she handles her loss stoically. For months she speaks wistfully of Gray Bunny, sometimes consoling herself and those around her by saying, "He'll come back later." A doll she has named Fairy Princess Ballerina steps in to fill the void. A revisionist at three, Grace fondly begins to recall her old friend as "White Bunny," a hue he never achieved.

Pink Cleats

One hot-pink soccer cleat, its scuffed toe poking out from under the rumpled bedclothes—all that remains after three satisfying but exhausting days of having my sixteen-year-old niece as a houseguest. I'm left wondering what inspired Erin to bring her cleats on this trip, a visit from her home in California to look at East Coast colleges. It took both of us to wrestle her overstuffed suitcase up the stairs and into my guest room. For all I know she had a soccer ball and goal in there too. What other clues to her growing-up self were tucked into that lumpy bag?

When Erin was little we were together often, even though we sometimes lived on opposite sides of the country; I traveled a lot for work in those days, and any time I could stretch a business trip into a visit, I did. We shared family times and invented our own adventures too—window shopping, tea at a café, stringing beads into jewelry. But then my brother and his family moved to Japan for three years. I'd seen Erin only twice since she became a teenager. Her life was so much bigger now, on the brink of expanding yet again as she made plans for college. How would we be with each other, I wondered before her visit. What would we talk about? I felt almost shy about seeing her again, having her stay in my house.

Within minutes of her arrival, I discover that soccer offers a window into her world. Erin's sentences are peppered with references to camps, coaches, yellow cards, and teammates. In my upstairs hallway, she dangles the bright pink cleats by their gray laces so I can admire them. "These are my favorites," she announces. Are they talismans for her journey, I wonder, or the opening line to a story she wants to tell? Did she pick them up on her travels to Singapore, or perhaps Hong Kong? She doesn't explain, she just goes back to the guest room and adds the cleats to the impressive assortment of belongings that has exploded out of her suitcase onto the bed and floor. I'm left to decipher the meaning behind the cleats while Erin deftly swaps text messages with friends in other time zones.

At the end of our first full day together, Erin sprawls across my sofa, twisting and twirling her long, auburn hair as she describes school projects she's led. Confidently, she tells me she's the one her classmates rely on to write, rewrite, or otherwise polish team presentations. "Good for you," I say. ("Be careful," I want to say, "there's a price to pay for being that girl.") I tell her about my recent decision to leave the company where I've worked since before she was born. We talk about finding meaning in work, and in school. She's eager for us to watch her favorite movie, *Newsies*; she just happens to have the DVD in her suitcase. We compare our different ways of being in the world: Erin feels lucky to have lived in many places, but doesn't really belong to any of them; I have always lived in the same place, give or take a few dozen miles, but relish the opportunities I've had to travel for work and for pleasure. We talk until we're both half-asleep.

For three days, we look at college campuses, explore Philadelphia, window shop, share meals, and visit with the nearby members of our clan. And then she's gone, as suddenly as she appeared. I call California to let her know she left one of her favorite cleats behind and to assure her that it's already on its way to her in the mail. She hasn't even missed it.

Diamond Earrings

For reasons I still cannot fully articulate, I decide to mark my forty-fifth birthday by buying myself a pair of diamond earrings. I've long since stopped waiting for anyone else to buy me diamonds, yet somehow I feel incomplete as a diamond-less woman of a certain age. I want to know how it feels to sparkle, to glint.

Most of my jewelry has more sentimental than monetary value. My favorite pieces remind me of somewhere or someone I've been: a silver necklace from Ireland, a bead bracelet from a pueblo near Santa Fe, blue topaz earrings to match the glacier I walked on in the Canadian Rockies. I've also kept school rings, pearls, and stickpins from my suit-wearing thirties, and a birthstone ring my parents gave me in grade school.

It takes several months—and a little coaching from my friend Luanne—to convince myself that I should buy the diamond earrings. Luanne is well-practiced at making fine-jewelry purchases, and she gladly accompanies me to her favorite jeweler one day on our lunch break. She helps me select my earrings from a glittering case while the jeweler hovers nearby, trusting one of his best customers to make the sale for him. Luanne suggests something with a bit of a design—the flower petals or the small teardrops, perhaps—but in the end she supports my choice of simple diamond studs. I think she understands I'm more interested in making a gesture than a statement.

When I reach my fiftieth birthday, I find I can count on one hand the times I've worn my diamond earrings. It turns out my life does not include many diamond-wearing occasions, something I never knew before. I get a postcard from the jeweler every time he has a sale. He has no way of knowing I won't be coming back.

I hold on to the credit card statement that records my diamond-earring purchase because it also records one of my favorite inside jokes: The purchase listed just below the earrings is a CD from a Joan Baez concert. The charge is to her record label, Diamonds and Rust, also the title of one of my favorite songs from her repertoire. Decades ago, Joan penned a somber ending to her ballad. I've always understood the song as acknowledging the cost of hard-earned—yet still precious—life lessons. But the last several times I heard her sing this song on stage, she deadpanned her way to an older, wiser, if less poetic, conclusion—a lyrical shrug of the shoulders about taking the diamonds, if they were still being offered.

Perhaps over time I'll rewrite my take on the diamonds too. For now, I like the way they sparkle in the gray velvet box where they mostly live; I open it occasionally, just to be sure they're still there.

Taking Inventory

I'm writing this backwards, I suppose. The diamond earrings were tucked away in a drawer long before Erin came to visit. Gray Bunny didn't disappear for some months after that. In fact, Erin and Gray Bunny crossed paths during the college-tour visit, although Grace did not have occasion to see the soccer cleats, which is too bad because she would have delighted in their utter pinkness.

Sometime between those events and now, I come across a small, well-worn teddy bear in the cedar chest in my guest room, a gift brought from Europe by my Uncle John's parents in the months before I was born. There's a photograph somewhere of the bear propped up in the crib of my nursery-to-be. I have no recollection of carrying this pale pink bear around with me or giving it a name. My earliest memory of the bear is seeing it tucked away in my mother's cedar chest for safekeeping. Because she saved it, I came to know it as a treasure. Eventually it moved from her cedar chest into mine. The pink has faded nearly to gray. Perhaps one day I'll offer the bear to Grace, as a reminder of, not a replacement for, her long-lost bunny.

Another day between then and now, I happen upon an ancient baseball glove in my attic, so creased with disuse that I have to pry it open to see the Willie Mays signature. I wonder why I've kept it for so long. I'd like to say it conjures up fond memories of my glory days as an outfielder, but unlike Erin, I never excelled at any sport, although I tried a few. The leather is worn with age, but the glove is barely broken in from use. Yet it's moved with me from place to place, a reminder of a time when it was almost novel for girls to play in a softball league; and of later co-ed games on summer nights with work friends from half a lifetime ago.

Like the Joan Baez song, my old possessions acquire new layers of meaning over time. If they hadn't bumped into Grace's bunny and Erin's cleats in my mind, I might not have given either of them a second thought when I opened the cedar chest for a blanket or climbed to the attic to stash an armful of old papers in a box. I don't think of these objects as necessary, and like my diamond earrings, perhaps they never were. Still, I keep them.

Or maybe it's the other way around. Perhaps Gray Bunny struck a chord because of the once-pink teddy bear stashed in my memory. Perhaps it seemed important to know why Erin's cleats made that cross-country trip because I can't explain my own attachment to a long-neglected baseball glove. In the end it doesn't matter because the bunny and the bear, the cleats and the glove, and even the diamond earrings all share one space in my thoughts now.

Three ages, three girls. What we treasure, what travels with us.

The Great Butter Caper of Chartres

The French playwright Jean Anouilh once said, "Everything in France is a pretext for a good dinner."

VISIONS OF FRENCH FOOD DANCED THROUGH MY MIND, prompted no doubt by my growling stomach, as the train pulled into Chartres. We were stopping there to rendezvous with the other half of our six-person traveling party and to move our body clocks ahead by six hours. The next day we would begin the real adventure—bicycling through the Loire Valley, staying in chateaux, and dining like royalty. Today we needed only to stay awake long enough to eat a meal that would compensate for the insults of airplane food and railway coffee.

A short taxi ride delivered us to the hotel, where our three fellow travelers already had checked in. They emerged from the dining room just as we arrived, looking fresher and better fed than us. We three had come from Philadelphia, while they had traveled from Detroit. Our noisy blend of reunions and introductions—some of us had never met—created a stir in the lobby.

As has frequently been my experience in France, we arrived in town just moments after the clock struck two, thereby forfeiting any chance at a freshly prepared midday meal. While the Detroit contingent lounged in their rooms, we strolled to the town center and settled for cafe au lait and pre-fab Croque Monsieur sandwiches, which tasted like the plastic they were wrapped in. Our dinner plans began to take on greater urgency—we'd been in France since dawn and had yet to experience the least little thrill over what we'd ingested.

Revived by the caffeine, if not the food, we set off to explore

Chartres. After gawking at the majestic Cathedral Notre Dame de Chartres from every possible angle on the outside, we tiptoed into the eight-hundred-year-old Gothic structure, awed by its history and scale. We explored the dimly lit cathedral, then emerged through a side door into dazzling sunlight and a rowdy procession of locals in brightly colored medieval garb. We followed jesters, clerics, ladies of the court, and musicians through narrow side streets to the town hall, where a small-scale carnival was in full bloom. Competing strains of music drifted from a bandstand and a carousel, and the inevitable smell of *frites* wafted over the crowd. As the medieval costumes melted into a sea of shorts and sundresses, we collapsed on a nearby lawn, laughing at the small part we had played in the festivities.

The French playwright Jean Anouilh once said, "Everything in France is a pretext for a good dinner." We'd seen Chartres in less than three hours, hardly enough time for this gem of a town, but surely enough pretext for a day that began where a red-eye flight left off. We walked back to the hotel to rendezvous with our friends and revive ourselves for the evening.

At 7:00 pm, all six of us set off in search of an early dinner. We needed a menu we could understand since I was the only one in the group who spoke French, and my skills were limited. We needed a restaurant that did not require reservations and would feed us sooner, not later. We wandered for a few blocks, scanning menus for words we recognized, peering into windows, checking opening times. In the end, we did not so much select a restaurant as it selected us by virtue of it being the first one we happened upon that was open.

Madame, in a crisp white blouse and dark calf-length skirt, greeted us formally inside the foyer and led us down a short flight of stairs into the small dining room. A bar with a large mirror for a backdrop dominated one wall. There were no more than twelve tables, each set neatly with silver and glassware for parties of two or four. The only natural light came from small, high windows nicely dressed in lace. The room had a homey feel, which was unmatched by the business-like demeanor of our prim, sixty-ish hostess, who was still trying to decide where to seat us.

We were the first guests that evening. Apparently, parties of six were unusual here, necessitating the rearrangement of several pieces of furniture by *Monsieur*, the bartender. And while there was no reason—at least up to this point—for our hosts to consider us "ugly Americans," we clearly were Americans on holiday, which made us somewhat suspect. From the brief exchange required to request a table for six, it was clear only French was spoken here. We sat at the newly configured table, as close as possible to the stairs. Important ground rules and subtle warnings were being telegraphed.

I was perhaps more sensitive to the signals than my companions. I could already see the six of us through *Madame's* eyes, and I understood why she might not have chosen to start her Saturday evening custom this way. I was keenly aware that it would fall to me to establish rapport and demonstrate that, American or not, we were capable of ordering a French meal in a dignified manner with only a modicum of assistance. I sensed from *Madame's* glances down the full length of her Gallic nose, as she distributed *cartes* and placed a wine list on the table, that nothing less than an all-out diplomatic effort would be required. She sighed audibly when we collectively declined a round of *aperitifs*.

Meanwhile, the dynamics of our newly assembled traveling party were beginning to emerge and, unfortunately, were leaning decidedly toward *Madame's* low expectations. Perhaps it was hunger, perhaps the day's heat, or perhaps we all had reached that dangerous, giddy, got-my-second-wind stage of jet lag. Whatever factors were at play, we were louder and bolder than we meant to be or, at least, than we ought to have been. This is not to say we were either very loud or very bold, but some of us had just met, others were catching up, and this was the official beginning of a trip we'd been planning for months. The energy level was high.

I nervously fingered my trusty travel dictionary under the skirt of the starched white damask tablecloth, concerned the situation might slip out of control. I was relying on the handy vocabulary section on dining to get us through the critical ordering of the meal, after which I assumed things would settle down at our table even as new guests arrived to distract *Madame*.

The wine list presented the first challenge. We agreed one red and one white would serve us well. However, my dictionary was no help in understanding the extensive (and expensive) list. In France, wines are listed by *terroir*, the region where the grapes are grown, not by the type of grape. We were clueless. We also were in the first blush of a trip to a foreign country, when the currency conversions don't come easily. *Madame* eavesdropped as we simultaneously did the math out loud and demonstrated our ignorance of French wines.

One of my new acquaintances, Allison, expressed her frustration over the lack of California vintages. *Madame* may not have spoken English, but she clearly recognized the word "California" in this context, and her back stiffened. Eventually, we settled on our two bottles, hovering just above the least expensive offerings in each category. *Madame* looked relieved when we signaled her over to order *du vin*. Anticipating the next set of challenges, I flipped frantically through the phrase book to decipher the many unfamiliar terms on the menu.

When in France, I have learned to trust the judgment of those who serve me food. I grasp at any scraps of advice offered by the *garçons* and *serveuses* who cringe as I mispronounce offerings from the *carte du jour*. Although this advice almost never comes in the form of an actual recommendation, the (frequent) indifferent shrug of a shoulder or the (rare) congratulatory smile has more than once determined my menu selections. I was fairly certain I would not be getting any helpful signals here.

Overhead, feet shuffled by the window. Occasionally two or more sets of feet stopped as their owners scanned the menu, not realizing that if they moved quickly, they could get dinner *and* a show here this evening. As we waited for our wine, we heard the door open, followed by footsteps as two new diners appeared. *Madame*, apparently delighted to see familiar (or at least French) faces, whisked them to the opposite corner of the room and seated them with great ceremony. They ordered *aperitifs* before she could proffer menus.

Soon other groups began to trickle down the stairs, mostly in twos and threes, never more than four to a party. *Madame* unceremoniously brought the wine to our table, leaving us to decant our own spirits. She could see that we were deeply immersed in our *cartes* and would not be rendering verdicts any time soon. She had other guests to attend to now, guests who spoke both *Français* and *vin* fluently. She looked at me as if to say, "*Bonne chance.*" I resumed my efforts to handle a barrage of questions from my friends.

For me the quality of a dining experience in France tends to be inversely proportional to the number of words exchanged in the process of ordering. Questions about how the *boeuf* has been raised or whether the head of the *poisson* might be removed before serving imply mistrust on the part of the diner. Requests to translate menu items do not often lead to satisfactory explanations and can evoke signs of impatience (or worse). Better to smile humbly and point to something you think you recognize than to flaunt your ignorance and cause the *garçon* to mime a duck paddling across a pond.

 I felt a great deal of pressure not to goof in interpreting the menu, fearing our already-strained relationship with *Madame* would be taxed further if I inadvertently mistook the name of an unsavory organ for an elegant sauce. I did my best to steer everyone toward safe selections—*poulet, boeuf,* or *poisson*—while discouraging them from ordering anything I could not translate with absolute certainty. I passed the phrase book around so the others could look up words discreetly, rather than revealing to everyone in the now-full dining room that we were rank amateurs at eating in France. I prayed fervently to Our Lady of Chartres to spare me from having to ask questions of *Madame*, dreading her glare as I struggled to make sense of the menu for my friends. But it was not to be helped; there were, despite my best efforts to discourage them, questions to be asked.

 Happily, I had underestimated *Madame* in this regard. She was a professional and, more importantly, the sort of French person who awards points for effort to foreigners who attempt to speak French. I spoke haltingly, sometimes resorting to a lame "*Qu'est-ce que?*" accompanied by a finger stabbing at the mystery words. With far more patience than she had exhibited thus far, she responded. Soon six orders were placed for first courses and entrées. *Madame* actually smiled as she collected our menus, no doubt pleased we had refrained from asking if the chef could make a cheeseburger.

 I felt a weight had been lifted from my shoulders. For me the evening now revolved around the delicate international relations campaign I was waging on behalf of my friends and my country, and I felt I'd just successfully negotiated an important treaty. Lulled into a false sense of security, I stashed the phrase book, sipped my wine, relaxed into my chair, and began to fantasize about that first tasty morsel of French cuisine.

 I studied the workings of the small restaurant. It appeared to be a two-person operation, starring *Madame* and, of course, *Monsieur*, the bartending, furniture-moving gentleman we'd already encountered. *Monsieur* was more than the bartender, as his absences from that post revealed. He may or may not have been the chef; at the least, he oversaw the kitchen. He disappeared through a swinging door for longer stretches as the dining room filled and orders were placed. *Madame* clearly was the front man in this operation. She greeted and seated each guest, took the orders, did all the serving. She was responsible for public relations and, as we were about to learn, she also was the designated disciplinarian, responsible for making and enforcing the rules of the establishment.

A few minutes after our orders were placed, *Madame* rewarded us with a heaping basket of bread. With all the fuss over the wine and menus, we hadn't even noticed we were breadless. The thick slices of crusty baguette were still warm. Oh, joy! We were in France, the wine was good, the bread was good, dinner surely would be good; in fact, life was good. What more could a girl ask for?

Well, for starters, a little butter. Allison was the first to notice there was none on the table. She must have been feeling sorry for me by then because instead of asking me to ask *Madame* for butter, she asked me how to make the request herself. Delighted someone else was willing to converse with *Madame* and confident this would advance our diplomatic cause, I offered up this simple phrase for Allison to try: *"Du beurre, s'il vous plait?"* She practiced a couple times, then managed to politely signal for *Madame's* attention. I sensed we were on the verge of a breakthrough.

When *Madame* approached, Allison spoke her line perfectly. *Madame*, a proud trustee of the French culinary tradition, hardly known for its stinginess with *le beurre*, offered a monosyllabic response: *"Non."* As she turned to walk away, Allison repeated her request, looking at me for assurance that she was saying the words correctly. She was. *"Non,"* came the reply once again. *Madame* looked at me as if to say, "Would you please translate *'non'* for your friend? She does not seem to understand." I wasn't sure I understood either, but I could see I was about to get stuck in the middle of a debate. I'd only met Allison a few hours earlier, but I already knew she was not accustomed to taking *"non"* for an answer. My acquaintance with *Madame* was even briefer, but I was equally certain she would hold her ground. I tried to intercede on Allison's behalf, justifying her request with the weak phrase *"pour le pain, s'il vous plait,"* my voice reaching for just the right inflection to suggest I was pleading for mercy.

Madame then launched into a *lecturette* I shall never forget. She looked at me the whole while, her eyes commanding me to translate her verdict and its explanation for Allison and the rest of my friends. Her tone was polite, but firm. Her voice was perhaps a bit louder than she realized. I don't pretend I caught every word of her dissertation, but I got enough to understand that *Madame* wished me to explain two important points to *mes amies:* First, the bread was perfectly good in its natural, unbuttered state; and second, *du beurre* would only fill us up prematurely, thereby detracting from our enjoyment of the sumptuous meals being prepared for us at this very moment. By the end of the discourse, I was on her side. *Madame* and I had sort of bonded during our question-and-answer session over the menu. Plus, she had a point—the bread *was* perfectly good *sans beurre.*

As I translated *Madame's* words, I watched Allison's eyes grow large with disbelief. She was learning a tough, un-American lesson. The customer is not always right, at least not when the customer challenges the judgment of a French *restauratrice.* Allison's face reddened. She looked at me as if a bad translation must be at the root of this misunderstanding. Was I certain *Madame* understood she simply wanted butter for her bread? Yes. Was I certain I'd understood *Madame's* reasons for denying her request? Not verbatim perhaps, but yes, well enough to know I'd captured the salient points.

Madame had been so emphatic in making her speech that everyone in the dining room now knew there was an incident brewing at the table nearest the door. I mentally calculated how many steps it would take to reach the safety of the street above. I half expected the French diners to rise as one and start singing *"Le Marseillaise,"* and if they had, I swear I would have joined in.

Everyone at our table had done their best to remain polite (though incredulous) as I translated Madame's long version of *"non."* Only Allison seemed to feel the bread was insufferable without butter. *Madame* obviously was in control here, and short of raiding the kitchen (which I thought Allison might just be capable of), we would not be having *du beurre* with our bread.

Even at that point there might have been a graceful ending to this tense moment. But Allison, who realized no butter would be forthcoming, could not help herself. She knew a couple other words in French, a phrase far more rudimentary than *"Du beurre, s'il vous plait?"* Glaring at *Madame*, who was in fact looking just a shade too triumphant, Allison spat out a sarcastic *"Merci beaucoup."*

With that, there was an explosion of laughter at our table, an unintended affront to our fellow diners, but an inevitable response to all that had transpired. Poor *Madame*. Had she stopped for a moment to consider the possible outcomes of denying us *du beurre* before serving up her lesson in the art of bread appreciation, it's possible she might have anticipated this disruption. It's even just the tiniest bit possible she might have relented and brought us an ounce or two of the precious substance, possibly requiring us to sign informed consent releases. But it all happened so quickly. She simply gave the best answer she knew to a question she perceived as impertinent. My efforts at diplomacy crumbled in front of my eyes, like the dry bread between my fingers.

The rest of the evening was blessedly uneventful. Allison recovered pretty quickly, although she continued to practice saying, *"Du beurre, s'il vous plait?"* throughout the meal—as we all did. Madame served our starters and then our entrées, somewhat coolly, although with no open hostility, mindful of her other patrons. We ate a very fine meal, an assortment of pleasing dishes, each of which had been prepared using more-than-ample quantities of *le beurre*, thereby reaffirming my belief that Madame was judicious, not stingy, with this particular staple. After dessert and coffee, we settled our debt and sleepily made our way back to the hotel. By morning, the great butter caper of Chartres seemed even sillier, almost surreal. Had Madame really refused to serve us butter with our bread? Impossible! Weren't we in France? Should we report this lapse to the authorities?

Not once for the rest of the trip did we need to ask for butter; it magically appeared at every meal. We ate breakfasts of fresh apricots, tangy yogurt, and baguettes. We had picnic lunches or simple meals in cafés as we pedaled our way from one chateau to the next. We ordered *aperitifs* and learned enough about French *terroirs* to bluff our way through book-length wine lists. We had sumptuous six-course dinners in honest-to-goodness castles, preceded by champagne-soaked receptions on terraces with breathtaking views. And everywhere we went, where there was bread, there was *du beurre*. Each time it seemed a most generous gift, an extravagance, almost superfluous, because Madame was never far from our minds.

One phrase dominated our days and nights: *"Du beurre, s'il vous plait?"* It became our rallying cry, as meaningful to us as *"Allons enfants de la patrie."* We greeted each other with it every morning. We shouted it from bicycles as we passed each other on quiet roads rimmed with sunflowers. We whispered it politely at dinners served beneath crystal chandeliers as we took turns spearing one, two, three little squares at a time to be sure not a single crumb of bread would go unslathered while we remained in France.

Dress Rehearsal • acrylic on canvas

Ghost Story

The man's performance is well underway now. The woman listens in disbelief as her coworkers roar at lines she has labored over, polished, and served up to the executive suite on a floppy disc.

SPONTANEOUS APPLAUSE RIPPLES THROUGH THE HOTEL ballroom in waves, a new one breaking before the last has even receded. Almost from the beginning the thousand or so people in the tiered banquet seats rise to their feet at frequent intervals, disrupting the official proceedings. The man on the stage doesn't mind these interruptions. From her seat in the midst of the audience, the weary woman in her late thirties with a clipboard in her lap watches as the final session of a weeklong sales meeting unfolds. In another hour she'll be on her way to the airport, heading for the quiet of her own apartment, where she will not have to share her bedroom with a steadily blinking laptop or don a plastic-sheathed name badge and wait in line to eat breakfast. She tries to focus on keeping her head up and her shoulders back, smiling and clapping in all the right places, which she already knows by heart.

If I could tell myself the story of how I got from there to here without going back to this scene, I would. I have avoided the return trip for many years. I know what waits inside the memory, and I'd rather not see myself as I was then, the weary woman with the clipboard in her lap, coaxing herself to sit through one more well-rehearsed speech.

The meeting represents a significant milestone for the man on the stage and the people in the room. The new product that is being launched was discovered in the US laboratories of the international pharmaceutical company where the woman has worked for most of the last ten years. It is the first such discovery to reach the market—a triumph for the smattering of scientists seated among the hundreds of salespeople who will soon be promoting the product. All week, people at the meeting have been talking as if the company is on the brink of something big, a breakthrough to the future. Despite a gnawing sense of dissatisfaction, which she is inclined to blame on the sleep deprivation that accompanies these meetings, the woman feels a twinge of pride in knowing her carefully chosen words have helped to frame this important moment for so many people. Also, she cannot deny a certain level of pleasure in hearing the closing speech delivered from the stage precisely as she heard it in her head while she was writing it. She listens as the speaker hits the right lines with emphasis, nails the punch points, and whips the willing audience into a frenzy, one sentence at a time. Of course, by now she's written so many speeches for this man that she knows how he speaks, he knows how she writes, and they rarely disappoint each other when he steps onto a stage.

Even as I sat there, I somehow already knew that this particular speech at this particular meeting would come to represent both the high point and the low point of my long career as a ghostwriter. For more than fifteen years, I had been editing articles and textbooks as a medical writer, producing anonymous company publications and announcements as a communications manager and—most recently and most ghostly of all—putting words into other people's mouths as an executive speechwriter.

The man's performance is well underway now. The woman listens in disbelief as her coworkers roar at lines she has labored over, polished, and served up to the executive suite on a floppy disk. She's written good speeches before, but never has she witnessed a response like this. The louder the audience cheers, the more she squirms in her seat. Then the scene takes a turn toward the surreal as the speaker's normally steady voice briefly wavers with emotion, a moment the woman has perhaps precipitated, but most definitely has not anticipated. She feels her cheeks burning as she accepts high fives from the men sitting on either side of her, friends who are in on her secret. "Did you just get him to cry? Wow, that's good," one of them whispers, perhaps a bit too loudly.

Unsuspecting colleagues shoot puzzled looks in their direction between cheers for the company president, who has quickly regained his composure and is now so caught up in the fervor that he is playing air guitar to the chorus of Bruce Springsteen's "Born in the USA," which has been inserted to neatly punctuate his remarks. For just an instant, the speaker goes off-script for his impromptu pantomime. The audience loves it, although most of them seem oblivious to the fact that there even is a script. From their seats, it's hard to tell that the rim of the stage is littered with Teleprompter monitors, making it possible for an experienced reader to address every corner of the room without dropping a line, missing a beat, or otherwise giving away the source of his unfaltering stream of sentences.

In the moment I felt invisible, but from my current vantage point I see myself clearly in that crowd on that day when the level of deception involved in bringing a speech to life at last seemed too great a burden to bear. Perhaps the speaker's emotion, prompted by a few lines of reflection on his first meeting as a young sales representative, struck a nerve. There he stood, the mighty president of the US division of a major pharmaceutical company, an achievement he could hardly have foreseen at the beginning of his career. And there I sat, handmaiden to the corporate machinery that cranked out one new product after another, quite possibly the last place in the world I would have expected to find myself at the beginning of my career.

To the woman's ears, the words themselves ring true—but then, they usually do. She likes writing speeches for this man because his style, like hers, is direct, and because he will only say words that he means, even if he hasn't thought of them on his own. Still, as he struts back and forth and confidently releases her words into the room, she feels disillusioned with the speaker, the speech, the audience, and most of all, the role she has carved out for herself in this charade.

She longs for someone to pull back the curtain, like Toto in *The Wizard of Oz*, and reveal the "magic" that allows the speech to be delivered so smoothly: a young man in a headset and the plain black clothes of a stagehand, lit only by the faint blue glow of a computer screen, feeds bite-sized nuggets of text into monitors for the man to read to his mostly unsuspecting audience. The woman allows herself the momentary pleasure of following this thread of thought to a place where the powerful man on the stage gestures nervously to a murmuring audience, bidding them, "Pay no attention to the man behind the curtain." But even as she lets her mind wander, she knows she cannot fool herself into thinking that what is upsetting her is the artifice playing itself out on (and behind) the stage, the sleight of tongue that allows the speaker to sound so sure of himself.

I didn't begrudge the man on the stage the words he spoke; after all, I had given them to him freely—or more precisely, swapped them for my ample salary. I didn't envy him for being the one on the stage. It wasn't about recognition or the lack of it, anymore. The problem, I realized, had nothing to do with the speech, the speaker, or anyone else in that vast ballroom but myself. Well, not myself exactly, but the faint outline of an earlier draft of myself, a draft I had inadvertently stuffed into a drawer or a box on my way to—what? A corporate sales meeting? That couldn't be right.

The woman slouches a few inches lower in her seat. For a minute or maybe two, she closes her eyes and allows the words to become no more than a blur. Her thoughts drift back to her first job after college, in a children's hospital, where she helped physicians write and publish papers in academic journals and textbooks and prepare speeches for conferences. She was so proud to carry a business card that proclaimed her to be a writer (a "medical writer," to be precise) that at first she didn't care that her work only ever appeared under other people's names. Just once had a doctor acknowledged—in writing—her supporting role in his success as an author. She'd rationalized away the anonymity of her work—at the hospital and later in a medical publishing house—as valuable years of apprenticeship, years in which she had honed her writing craft, albeit within the structural confines of the scientific method and the language, mostly, of medicine.

Later, when she took a public relations job at the pharmaceutical company, she was certain she was on her way to becoming a "real" writer, not the silent partner who shaped or tweaked other people's words. The path seemed clear at the time: after two or three years of business experience, she'd be ready to hang out her shingle as a freelance writer and editor, earning enough to carve out time, at last, for her own writing, whatever that meant; she would parlay her behind-the-scenes success into the literary life she'd always imagined. Now, all these years later, she finds herself at a loss to explain how she's come to be in this empty place that is full of her words, each one of which betrays her as it enters the now-raucous room.

Her business card no longer identifies her as a writer but as an employee communications manager. The men at the top of the organizational chart don't seem to care what her business card does or doesn't say as long as she feeds them a steady stream of well-crafted speeches, written announcements, and company publications. Above all else, they value her as a writer, an irony that is not lost upon her in the rare moments when she lets such thoughts intrude, or when they come unbidden, like now.

It was a chilling discovery to see my situation so clearly in the light of that dim ballroom. As the words coming from the stage approached a climax, I recalled a recent conversation with a sales manager. "This sounds so much like me I would swear I wrote it myself, if I didn't know better. How do you do that?" My response made him laugh: "Don't you know you're all just fictional characters who live in my head? I conjure up your voices as I need them." I left his office thinking I'd hit a new low in my long-running game of self-sabotage. If there were any literary stripes to be earned as a speechwriter, they probably did relate to the ability to write for other people in voices that were true for them. Somehow, though, what I did for these men felt more like a clever party trick than a writerly skill.

In the ballroom, the audience rises for one last burst of applause, and for a fleeting instant, the woman feels grateful to be flanked by friends who know her role in this highly orchestrated affair. Then one of the men cheers softly, "Author! Author!" and she suddenly wishes she could vanish into thin air. Mercifully, his chant is swallowed up by the din, although it will haunt her waking thoughts for months to come. The other man leans toward her and says, "His lips are moving, but I can hear your voice." She knows he is wrong, though, because no one—not even the woman herself—has heard *her* voice, her own authentic voice, in all the years she's made a living by giving her words away.

The final, long ovation fades into a swell of upbeat walk-out music, and the crowd scrambles noisily down the wide steps and toward the exits. The woman takes her time reaching under the chair to retrieve her purse and the heavy laptop case that will remain tethered to her right shoulder until she settles into a window seat for the long flight home. The man on the stage basks in the glow of his well-received oration, surrounded by a clutch of vice presidents and a dozen other well-wishers. By tacit arrangement, the woman does not join in this post-speech, locker-room-like celebration, sparing everyone involved a small measure of potential awkwardness. The proud president does not need to be reminded that the flattery being directed toward him could just as easily be deflected to a mid-level manager with a clipboard under her arm. And the woman doesn't dare draw too close to the blinding lights that still illuminate the stage, for fear of being mistaken again for a mere ventriloquist.

Still, she knows that in a week or so, she will be summoned to a conference room, along with the others who worked so hard to make this meeting successful. She dreads the small ceremony that will unfold as each of them is presented with a token of appreciation from the management team: an elegant pen—a Waterman or Mont Blanc, no doubt—which she will add to the collection she has stashed at the back of a desk drawer. "Insult to injury" is how it feels each time she accepts another pen, even though she knows the gesture is well-intentioned and that it's no one's fault but her own if she allows the pens to remain unused.

The woman steps slowly down the tiers of banquet chairs, which are already being collected and stacked toward one side of the room. She lingers briefly near the exit, willing herself to memorize this scene, to memorize the feeling of being already gone from a room that is still alive with the echo of her words. She knows she has written herself into this unhappy corner. She has to believe there is still a ghost of a chance that she will write her way back out of it.

I couldn't have known it then, but many years and many more speeches would come and go before I finally removed one of those pretty pens from its silk-lined box, unscrewed the cap, inserted the cartridge and began to write words in a voice I knew to be my own. The man on the stage had long since retired, the product we launched that day had proven to be a commercial disappointment, and the company as we knew it had ceased to exist in the wake of a merger. Eventually I wriggled out of the speechwriting role, and later still I made my escape from the corporate world. Still, my thoughts have drifted through that ballroom many times in the intervening years, although until now I've not let them linger there for long. It's possible, I suppose, that what I thought I discovered that morning didn't dawn on me until later, until after I'd left that life behind me for good.

Dear Phillies

*I've got Phillies t-shirts that are older than eighteen. I mean
I was wearing hot pants back when they were a new thing.*

DEAR PHILLIES,

I know the deadline for applications for ballgirl positions for the 2012 season has long since passed, and I know you explicitly asked for a video to support each written application. But I'm not sure a video would help my chances of becoming a ballgirl, even if I had the technological wherewithal to videotape myself looking all perky and dodging ground balls while proclaiming the merits of adding me to your lineup.

So please, allow me to introduce myself to you and present my considerable qualifications, based on your requirements, in writing. If you still require a video, I'll be happy to comply, but I am confident it won't come to that.

Public Relations Skills—Have you taken communications, broadcasting, or public speaking classes?

I would venture to say you've never had a ballgirl with such extensive public relations skills and experience. From my college days as an ambassador for our fair city at the information desk at the Philadelphia International Airport through nearly two decades as a public affairs professional for a major international corporation, I've seen it and done it all. I may not be your first choice when it comes to posing for photo ops, but I can organize press conferences and photo shoots, write press releases, and field media questions.

I've handled crisis communications and community relations. I've planned major events, written speeches for busy executives, produced newsletters, and for years, was a card-carrying member of the International Association of Business Communicators. Just don't ask me to "tweet," OK?

Must be Athletic—Softball experience a plus

I have never been accused of being athletic, nor am I likely to be. However, back in the Dark Ages before Title IX, I did play softball in a girls' league in the summers between fifth and eighth grades. As a young adult, I played in pick-up games with work friends. I wouldn't say I played well, mind you, but let's be honest about the level of athleticism required to succeed as a ballgirl. Could I get out of the way of ground balls and fly balls? Absolutely. Would I be able to bend over, pick up a dead ball, and hand it to a kid sitting in the first row? Without question. Do I know the difference between a ball that's in play and one that's foul? You bet.

Anyone who ever watched me play softball can attest to the fact that I have a real knack for getting out of the way of balls heading in my direction; in fact, I consider this to be my best-honed softball skill. My favorite softball position was always short field—between second base and right field—because there was always someone else nearby to call me off (and mostly, they did). I know it gets a little trickier when you have to simultaneously collapse a folding chair and get out of the way of a ball that's in play, but please, do not underestimate my instincts for self-preservation. Did I mention I still have a glove? And it's nearly as good as new.

From my grade-school days with the Kedron Youth Association, in the near suburbs of Philadelphia, I learned that even if you didn't play well, you could still look good. Or try, anyway. Girls' uniforms back then were decidedly ugly; ours featured boxy, short-sleeved, white cotton blouses (which had to be ironed) embroidered with a green "KYA." The tops were worn out and over—never tucked into—drab green, knee-length shorts (which also had to be ironed). Truly, my Catholic-school uniform was more flattering than my softball get-up. Still, my mother was determined I should look as good as I might for softball, even though I was mostly a benchwarmer/cheerleader. In addition to all the ironing she had to do (my sister was also a benchwarmer on the same team), she insisted on setting my hair in pin curls on the eve of every game, ignoring the fact that only a wisp or two had a chance of peeking out from under my stiff green cap.

I am confident the attention to grooming associated with my early softball experience would serve me well as a Phillies ballgirl.

Knowledge of the Game of Baseball

I know and *love* the game of baseball, despite and because of the fact that I am a lifelong Phillies fan. I grew up listening to baseball on the radio, a great way to learn the fine points of the game because it forced me to picture what was being described and allowed me to internalize the rhythms of the game, its sounds, its silences. (Remember when baseball games were punctuated with the sounds of silence?) I still like to catch an entire game that way, once in a while, for the memories it evokes—family car rides, staticky transmissions on the beach in Wildwood, and going to games with my grandfather, who watched every play with a transistor radio pressed closed to his ear. I relish the challenge of tuning into a game that's underway and figuring out, just from the tone of the announcers' voices, where things stand for the home team before the inning ends and they give me a score.

Once, back in the early 1990s, I smuggled a radio into a fancy dinner with the top brass of the company I worked for. I was supposed to be flattered because I'd been invited to a special banquet for up-and-comers, but really I was annoyed because the Phillies were playing a late-September game that mattered, and I had to keep dashing off to the ladies room, where the reception was really lousy, to check on the score. The guys at my table were glad I was there.

I speak fluent baseball, and I love the language of the game, especially the verbs associated with hitting: to lace, to line, to loop, to dribble, to squirt a ball into play. It makes me smile every time a broadcaster says the Phillies have "put up a crooked number" in an inning, or better yet (though far less frequently) "put up a snowman."

I know what it means to hit for the cycle and what a rare accomplishment that is. I can recall two perfect games by Phillies pitchers in my lifetime; okay, the first one I can't exactly recall, and I was out of town for the second one, but my father called to tell me about it just seconds after the final out was recorded. I cannot pretend to have memorized every obscure rule of the game—although I like knowing they are there—but let's just say you'd never trip me up on the basics.

I remember when Veterans Stadium was brand-spanking new. For all the years that concrete bowl passed for a baseball park, I was mostly a denizen of the zoo-ish 700 level, except for the summer of '71 when I was a Phillies Straight A student and scored a bunch of free tickets on the 500 level, along with a nifty pencil case, ruler, and other school supplies.

Somewhere in my attic I still have the kazoo I played in the late '70s as part of a Phillies crowd that made it into the *Guinness Book of World Records* for the largest-ever all-kazoo orchestra. I have yellowed news clips from the 1980 World Series that I cannot part with. I used to go to double-headers on purpose, so I could watch twice as much baseball in a single sitting. One of my prize possessions is a two-headed bobble-head figurine of the golden-gloved Richie (Whitey) Ashburn and the silver-tongued Harry (the K) Kalas.

I was present for two of the final three games at The Vet in 2003. I braved snow flurries and raw winds to get my first look at Citizens Bank Park on opening weekend in 2004. I've weathered impressive rain delays and scorching heat waves over the decades, endured sunburns and nearly been frostbitten, all to cheer on my beloved Fightin' Phils, mostly during seasons that were not particularly memorable. I was proud to be among the faithful in attendance on the fateful day in 2007 when the Phillies recorded their world-leading 10,000th franchise loss. And I was lucky enough to be there on those *two* fateful nights in October 2008—I still get goose bumps remembering the thrills and the chills—when we won the World Series in a Game 5 that took about fifty hours to complete.

Flexible Schedule—Must be willing to work early AM, nights, weekends, and holidays

Trust me, if your decision to hire me as a ballgirl comes down to a question of scheduling, I will clear my calendar and set up a cot in Ashburn Alley if need be.

Must be eighteen years of age

When I first read this on your website, I thought it might be a deal breaker. Then I read the fine print and saw that you meant "*at least* eighteen years of age." Whew! I've got Phillies t-shirts that are older than eighteen. I mean I was wearing hot pants back when they were a new thing. Not that I thought the Phillies would be an ageist organization; after all, you hired Charlie Manuel to manage the team when he was already into his second decade as an AARP member. Then you signed Jamie Moyer as a starting pitcher when some people thought he was past his prime. And those moves turned out pretty well for everyone involved, didn't they?

Anyway, if you're willing to consider a ballgirl who is more or less (OK, more, but just by a few years) a contemporary of Jamie's, I'm your girl. Although we might want to discuss the merits of "ballwoman" as a more appropriate title.

I hope I've convinced you I would make a great Phillies ballgirl. Again, I know my application is late, but one of those sweet young things you've already hired based on her airbrushed photo and her adorable video is bound to suffer a real sports injury some time during the season, and when that happens, I will be ready to step in and fill her cleats.

Phaithfully yours,
Eileen

Independence Day

> *It seemed funny that the four of us—all second-generation Americans who'd grown up within miles of the Liberty Bell—had had to travel so far from home to truly experience the Fourth of July.*

I LEANED BACK INTO DEEP, SILKY CUSHIONS, STILL SAVORING the tang of mint and cilantro on my tongue. The soup was beginning to warm me from the inside out, taking away the chill of a drizzly afternoon. The sign over the archway that led into this nearly deserted courtyard in an otherwise-bustling quarter of the city read "Casablanca." In our quest for a memorable meal on the last day of our journey, we'd opted for one of the outdoor, bead-curtained canopies with low, plush sofas, even though we would have been much warmer at an inside table, and it would have been far easier to reach the table, not to mention the soup. Each time a fez-topped waiter entered our little tent, the beads swayed and clacked and a fresh wave of pungent aromas wafted toward us. It never seemed to be the same waiter twice; we wondered if they were taking turns because they had no other customers.

The food—which, except for the soup, we'd eaten with our fingers—and the trance-inducing music being broadcast throughout the neighborhood made the illusion almost complete. We had, in fact, followed the music through a tangle of cobbled streets to find our Casablanca. Never mind that my three new friends and I were washing down our Moroccan feast (if "cattle salad"—strips of grilled steak over couscous and greens—is in fact a Moroccan dish and not just a bad translation) with American beer in honor of the date, July 4th. It's not like we were in Morocco. No, we were in the heart of Prague, in the Czech Republic, where we could just as easily have celebrated Independence Day in TGI Friday's or Pizza Hut, then popped into a Dunkin' Donuts for dessert.

But for our penultimate meal, just a few hours ahead of a more traditional Czech dinner with a set menu featuring venison, we'd decided to add one last layer of cross-cultural experimentation to our collective memories of Prague. What was a Moroccan restaurant doing in the middle of Prague anyway? Was it an homage to the fictional Czech hero Victor Laszlo? Or had the Moroccans invaded Prague along with America and most of Europe once the free-market economy had begun to take root? And was this culinary discovery any stranger than the disco party on an after-dinner cruise down the Vltava River that we'd experienced the night before or the surreal black-light marionette interpretation of *Yellow Submarine*—dialogue in Czech, soundtrack in English—we'd stumbled upon earlier in the week?

As part of a group of mid-career American graduate students from the University of Pennsylvania who for a week had been exploring this beautiful, sometimes eccentric maze of a city and its surrounding countryside, my friends and I had been embarrassed by the ubiquitousness of American "culture" in Bohemia. It seemed to clash horribly with the elegant profile of the castle that towered above the city, reminding us of Prague's rich and noble history. It was beyond ironic that every tourist map was dotted with golden arches while the words "site of former statue of Stalin" still haunted one high hill nearly forty years after the statue itself had been toppled.

Yet the dozens of businesspeople, academics, and government workers who had met with our seminar class all week could hardly contain their enthusiasm over the transformations that were taking place across Eastern Europe as foreign businesses moved in, opened shop, and infused much-needed funds and jobs into a newly capitalist society. Prague was the pulsing heart of a country very much in the midst of self-discovery, mostly driven by the passions of people still in their twenties and thirties. People older than that had generally taken a step or two back; they were happy to participate but not at all certain how to lead the charge in a world they no longer recognized.

While we waited for coffee, Maureen, Joe, Dan, and I compared the treasures we'd purchased that morning as we'd poked through a Saturday street market, made one last sweep through the shops around Old Town Square, and strolled among the makeshift stalls on the Charles Bridge: garnet jewelry, marionettes, colorful glass goblets, a pastel drawing, and—the largest purchase of all—a small crystal chandelier for Maureen's foyer. We congratulated ourselves on having collected authentic Czech souvenirs while avoiding the high-priced designer shops that had sprung up just off the square, the same shops we could find at home (tomorrow), in Philadelphia, if we were so inclined.

It seemed funny that the four of us—all second-generation Americans who'd grown up within miles of the Liberty Bell and had lived through the summer-long extravaganza that was the US Bicentennial celebration in 1976—had had to travel so far from home to truly experience the Fourth of July, the sense of being there at the beginning of history in a country that was inventing itself while the world watched with interest, lending seemingly boundless moral and financial support.

I'm not sure I ever fully tasted freedom until that rainy Saturday when I toasted my own nation's birthday in a Moroccan restaurant with a glass of *pivo* (the only Czech word I can recall all these years later) in a newborn-ancient land that only recently had escaped from the clutches of communism. It tasted sweet—and a bit exotic too.

Our coffee cups were drained, our fingers were growing cold, and we each had a lot of packing to do before dinner. We flagged the first fez we spotted and for one last time amused ourselves by saying, "Czech, please."

The Field Beyond the Field Below • acrylic on canvas

Shifting Landscapes

Being with this group reminded me of that earlier self and made me want to find her again and introduce her to these good people.

THE FIRST PHOTOGRAPH I TOOK WAS AT THE RUIN OF A Catholic church somewhere between the airport in Shannon and our cottages in Ballyvaughan, County Clare. One of my new traveling companions had convinced her husband and another man to hoist her high enough to touch a figure carved in stone above what remained of the entrance, sure it would bring her luck. The figure was a Celtic god or goddess, maybe two feet high and a foot across, with a curtain of ivy tickling its left side. A primitive, pagan symbol, more melting snowman than saint. In the picture, the woman's right hand just brushes the left foot of the stony deity, while her feet are tightly gripped by the two men below.

That photograph would prove to be emblematic of the trip—Celtic and Christian themes woven tightly together, people lifting each other up in every way, the stony surfaces of western Ireland offering up ancient secrets. And me with my camera—sometimes off to the side, sometimes in the picture—watching events unfold and hoping to make sense of it all.

But my favorite photograph from those ten days shows a group of soggy pilgrims in bright rain gear, one nearly indistinguishable from the next in the mist, hoods raised and hats on, plodding up a rocky hill in Connemara.

I like to believe my journey away from the corporate world began in earnest beside a little stream on the day I captured that foggy image, although a casual inventory of my bookshelves before the trip would have revealed I'd been inching my way toward the exit sign for quite some time, at least mentally. Among the books that had helped me cope or supported my case for leaving were: *Orbiting the Giant Hairball: A Corporate Fool's Guide to Surviving With Grace*, by Gordon Mackenzie; *Making a Life, Making a Living*, by Mark Albion; *Composing a Life*, by Mary Catherine Bateson; and the well-worn and much-highlighted book that had led me to that little stream, *The Heart Aroused: Poetry and the Preservation of the Soul in Corporate America*, by David Whyte.

I first heard Whyte speak at a business conference in 1998. He talked about how difficult it is for people in modern organizations to bring themselves fully into the workplace; he described the many ways we find to leave parts of ourselves—often the brightest, most creative parts—safely outside the office for fear of having them damaged or even destroyed. But he also offered hope—and evidence from work he'd done with many companies—of finding ways to invite the best parts of people back into the workplace, to the benefit of individuals as well as their employers.

I bought the book and read it twice in no time at all. I understood only too well the challenges Whyte described. I'd been holding parts of myself away from my work for as long as I could remember. I no longer knew if I'd been protecting those parts somewhere deep inside myself, or if they'd turned to stone or gone to ruin. By going to Ireland, I'd hoped to shake them loose.

In 1987, the year I went to work in the public relations department of a pharmaceutical company, the movie *Broadcast News* was released. I loved Jane Craig, the network news producer played by Holly Hunter, the go-to girl everyone relied on to get the job done, meet every deadline, make everyone else look good. On the surface, at least, she had it all together. But what I liked best about her was the funny, sad little ritual that launched her into each day: unplugging the phone and allowing herself to—no, making herself—cry out loud, for about thirty seconds. I'd never done that, but even in 1987, I'd recognized the impulse behind it.

By early 1999, I was an older version of Jane Craig, still waiting for that flash-forward scene where I'd figured out how to have a career, have a life, and take better care of myself. At least on the surface, I, too, looked to be successful. I was still at the same company, now as the manager of US employee communications.

I had succeeded in the business environment almost in spite of myself; I'd only intended to stay for a couple of years on my way to a freelance writing career. Yet there I was, about to complete a master's degree in organizational dynamics at an Ivy League university, caught up in two international working committees that had me bouncing back and forth between the East Coast and Europe, taking conference calls in my pajamas at both ends of the day, depending on where I happened to be. I was a go-to girl, a problem-solver, someone who could always be counted on to work late and craft the memos, the speeches, the broadcast voice-mail messages that made other people look good, that made sense of the company's news.

But below the surface I was a mess. I was dissatisfied with myself for the kind of work I was doing, but I couldn't stop doing it for long enough to imagine what I might do next. Through my graduate studies, I had discovered things about myself—and my relationship to work—that made me dislike not only my job but who I was in that role. To top it all off, the company was in the throes of a corporate merger, which had increased my workload exponentially. Despite my best intentions to avoid getting caught up in the fray, I'd let myself be badly battered all through that spring and summer by ugly politics, a one-sided army of consultants, and other stresses from the merger. And while I kept telling myself I had to find a way out of there, I also had a dozen ways of rationalizing why I needed to stay, what only I knew or only I could do that would make a difference to the new company and its employees.

Assuming, of course, that the new management team wanted me to stay, which was not a foregone conclusion. I had politely declined an invitation to be interviewed for a new role heading up global employee communications in London, a position I had lobbied to have created before the merger was announced. The likelihood of my being offered a comparable leadership role in the US business was slim, although I knew I would be interviewed for that position just after I returned from Ireland.

So by the time I arrived in the village of Ballyvaughan in September 1999 on a trip led by David Whyte—a trip described as "Poetry, Myth and Music for the Soul"—I was exhausted, sad, and in dire need of something, although I would have been hard pressed to say just what. I guess I hoped that by going to Ireland—where my grandparents all were born and where I had been only once before—I might catch my breath and maybe catch a glimpse of my future.

"Mystics," David called the merry band of about thirty travelers who assembled around a cluster of thatched-roof cottages near the bay on that first evening. Some days "mist-ics" would have been just as apt, as we slogged through drizzle and fog and stumbled over the moonscape of the limestone-clad region known as the Burren. Our itinerary included visits with literary, musical, spiritual, and environmental-activist friends of David's who lived in Clare or the surrounding counties; sometimes they came to us, other times we went to them—on foot, in vans, by ferry, or on bikes, sometimes all of the above in a single day. Our home base consisted of a cluster of "Irish-Rent-a-Cottages"—whitewashed, thatched-roof impersonations with limited modern amenities.

A few days into the trip, we drove north to Connemara where we were greeted at the roadside by a tall, burly man with a scraggly beard who looked more like a farmer than an internationally regarded poet and philosopher. In the few minutes it took John O'Donohue to welcome us to Connemara and introduce us to the landscape he'd grown up in, I decided he had the loveliest voice and the most elegant manner of stringing words together that I'd ever encountered. Each word was part whistle, part lilt, with perfect enunciation, even through his thick brogue.

Up we climbed through the Connemara fog, a trickle of brightly colored rain gear—reds and yellows, blues and greens—snaking up the slippery trace of a path, aiming for a tiny chapel tucked into the side of Mamean Mountain. At John's behest we walked in silence for the hour or so it took to reach our stopping point. The quiet gave me a chance to think about this group of relative strangers, some of whom already felt like good friends. I wasn't sure I belonged in the midst of these pilgrims. I somehow thought that people more like me—people who worked in big companies and were struggling to make sense of themselves in those challenging human landscapes—would have signed up for this trip, hoping to once again have their hearts aroused. Instead, I found myself surrounded by poets, philosophers, and spiritual adventurers, only a few of whom had first-hand knowledge of corporate America.

Long ago I'd written poems too, and some of them had even been published. Being with this group reminded me of that earlier self and made me want to find her again and introduce her to these good people. I was far less comfortable introducing them to my forty-year-old self. I wasn't sure how she would be received by so many free spirits, lifelong hippies, and New Agers, most of whom hailed from the western United States. I imagined I seemed to them like a typical uptight East Coaster, probably a sellout. How could they know how hard I had worked to avoid becoming a corporate creature, a ladder climber? I wanted them to see that underneath my assumed identity in the business world, I too was a poet, a seeker. I wanted to believe that about myself again too.

So in those first days in Clare, as we'd gathered around the large wooden table in our cottage, enjoying tea and freshly baked brown bread for breakfast; as we'd rattled around the stony hills in our rented vans; and as we'd combed the countryside in search of secret, sacred places, I found myself offering up a string of excuses for my current self:

"I'm just on the brink of changing jobs, and I'm trying to figure out what to do next."

"In a few weeks I'll probably be leaving the corporate world for good."

"I just had to finish my master's program first."

"I've been so busy with work and school that I'm still living in an apartment. As soon as I buy a house, I'll make my move."

Not that anyone had accused me of anything shameful or asked me to apologize for how I made my living. But seeing myself in relief against the backdrop of these people had made me feel even worse about the career choices I had (or hadn't) made, the ways I had allowed my identity to get mixed up with the work I did, even as I struggled to convince myself that what I did was quite different from who I knew myself to be.

In addition to what felt like an embarrassing business resume, I couldn't hold a candle to the elaborate spiritual journeys some of my new friends had experienced. I had been practicing just the one religion—Roman Catholicism, the Irish variety—my entire life, while others in the group had dabbled in assorted eastern religions; had spent time with the Dalai Lama; regularly consulted with shamans, spiritual advisors, and crystal healers; or were experts on mystics like Meister Eckhart and Saint Hildegard. I knew a thing or two about Celtic folklore and the little people, mind you; in fact, I was a relative expert in Irishness compared with most of the group. But I found myself keeping company with people who collected spiritual experiences in much the same way I collected teapots.

Even my body felt wrong. I know I wasn't the only one there who didn't have an advanced yoga practice and had never experienced meditation, but at times I found myself feeling that way. Others flexed and stretched their supple limbs on the lawn outside our cottages without the least self-consciousness or easily slipped into trances in the middle of stony fields, while the tight little fist I had knotted myself into struggled to unclench itself even for sleep.

Still, no one seemed to hold any of this against me. Just by virtue of showing up in Ballyvaughan, we all had been welcomed into each other's lives, and we all had identified ourselves as pilgrims, however varied our quests. There was something truly extraordinary about how open the members of this *ad hoc* community were, especially in contrast with the mean-spirited, hostile behavior I'd been experiencing at work since the merger. I liked being lost in the mist with these people and under the cover of silence that John O'Donohue had imposed on our climb. I marveled at how much I already knew about them, how intimate our conversations had been.

Jill was about my age and had recently done something I couldn't imagine: she'd left the job where she'd worked for sixteen years without knowing what she would do next. She had given herself the gift of time to thoughtfully make her next move.

Jim was retired but seemed to understand precisely where I was stuck. "Your next job doesn't have to be perfect," he'd said one day as we ambled through a field. "It just has to be a deliberate step away from what you're doing now, from what you don't like doing."

Lillian told me that on this trip she was paying particular attention to "the spaces in between"— literal and metaphoric—and I found myself drawn to talk with her. In the Burren, it was easy to find jumping-off points for this theme—plants poking up through cracks between rocks, light playing over ruins where roofs and walls had gone missing, clouds dramatically splitting open as they scurried across the sky. The seed of an idea perhaps slipped into a crack in my mind during my conversations with Lillian, although it would be a long while before it saw the light of day.

Maura was writing a novel on top of being a journalist, and she encouraged me to begin my own writing too, as if it were something I could take up as easily as knitting. My roommate Laurie was a wife, a mother, a nurse, *and* a published poet. Larry was an environmental scientist who wrote poems inspired by nature. From this trio—and others in the group—I began to see the possibilities of being "a writer and . . . "—a new way of thinking about myself in relation to work.

I had been writing, if only to myself, since I'd arrived in Ireland. The challenge, I knew, would be keeping that up when I got home. But home was still far away, and here I was in soggy, boggy Connemara, walking in silence with others who had somehow managed to find their own voices, regardless of whatever else they did.

We reached the top of the hill and huddled together against a rough wall of rock that sheltered the tiny Chapel of Saint Patrick. With half-frozen fingers, we unwrapped the sandwiches we'd packed in Ballyvaughan. As we ate, we began to speak again, tentatively at first, hushed words breaking through the long silence and into the bone-chilling rawness of the day. While we stood there, a heavy mist—or had we climbed straight into a cloud?—rolled in and erased the stony landscape we'd just been through, providing John with the perfect opening for a little talk—or a "blasht," as he and David liked to say—on the highly questionable "thereness" of the Connemara landscape and its relation to our own interior landscapes and geographies.

"We're not meant to know who we are," John said into the foggy air, in a voice that could only be called a mighty whisper. "We're meant to sense the landscape within and what's going on there." He spoke of frontiers and "undulating contours of narrative"—in Connemara and in our lives.

"It can be difficult," he said, "to know which version of a landscape or which version of your own story is true, considering how the elements keep playing with each other, making it hard at times to distinguish the bog from the granite, even though you were certain of which one it was just now when you were walking through it."

I felt like these words were aimed directly at me, though of course they weren't. I had pulled a small notebook out of my backpack, and I jotted down as much of what John was saying as

I could capture. I was absolutely at a loss to know which version of my own story was true: Was I a "real" writer wasting her time in corporate communications, or was that just a myth? Would I sabotage or save myself if I walked away from a communications career after all the time I'd invested in learning the field and earning my credentials? Was I afraid to become more successful in the business world or afraid I'd already climbed as high as I ever would? And how would my story change if I wasn't offered a job in the merged company—a possibility that loomed in the weeks ahead, one I couldn't figure out how to "spin," even in my own mind. Part of me wanted to let someone else decide what I should do next; part of me felt I had to own that decision myself, or stay stuck, even if I was lucky enough to be turned loose.

David had been telling us since we'd arrived that self-compassion is essential, and John reinforced this idea by reminding us how hard it can be to make your way in the world. They both spoke of "intentionality"—how important it is to be mindful of your own life, your own self, your own choices. I thought about the courage my grandparents had shown in leaving Ireland and everything they'd known to find their futures in America. And now I was back here as a tourist, worried about leaving a *job*? I understood what a privilege it was—a privilege I owed in part to those same grandparents—to have the luxury of looking for meaning in work, of choosing a career path. Did I owe it to them to make a good choice, or just to myself?

After John's "blasht," down the hill we stumbled through the wet grass and rock, almost back to the spot where we'd started. We were a noisy crowd on the descent, chattering in small groups, often above the roar of John's booming laughter. He stopped us just shy of the road where we'd met him, beside a lively stream we'd stepped over on the way up. He shushed us all again, growing more serious than he had been since the top of the hill.

"I want each of you to look around and find a stone," John instructed—an easy assignment in that place—"then gather yourselves around the water." He waited as we collected our stones, some of us picking up random pebbles resting at our feet, others searching the mossy ground for one with the perfect heft or smoothness.

"Now, I invite you each to think of something in your life that you want to let go of, some burden—large or small—that needs to be released. Think of the stone in your hand as that burden, and when you feel ready, release it into the stream."

As much as I'd enjoyed our time with John, my initial reaction to this ritual was just to play along, because it felt a bit contrived, a little too self-helpish for my taste. I'd felt so vulnerable in group situations in recent months at work that I wasn't sure how much of me I wanted to dredge up here in the bog, in front of an audience, or how emotional I might become if I did dredge something up. I knew I needed healing as much as anyone on that hillside, but being both Irish and Catholic, for me that was a private matter.

I had been perfectly content to let poems and words and music wash over me and rinse away the layers of anger and frustration I'd been experiencing all summer. I was more than willing to open myself up to the magic of an Irish landscape and the metaphors offered up by mist and stone, sun and rain. I was far less comfortable with spontaneous displays of spirituality—even those instigated by an erstwhile Catholic priest—and I was especially leery of group rituals because of the artificial "bonding" activities that had been imposed on me during the merger.

Still, I didn't want to reinforce my own sense of not belonging with the others on this trip, so I poked around for a stone to drop in the stream, intending only to mime the act of letting go of anything more substantial. I watched for a minute as my new friends dropped their stones, some gently and others with a splash. Then something I couldn't name took over—maybe the Irish landscape, maybe the earnest people scattered around me, maybe a gentle nudge from one of my ancestors. All at once, I knew what I wanted to release into the cold, clear water at my feet. I still didn't fully believe in the gesture, but I managed to suspend my skepticism long enough to give it a chance.

For months I'd been clinging to an idea of how my work had mattered to the people in my company before the merger and what that meant about who I was in that company and, to a lesser degree, in the larger world. I knew the old organization had already ceased to exist, and it was futile to try to hold onto it. All summer I'd been letting go by degrees. I kept reminding myself that I had vowed to find a way out of the corporate world once I finished school. But the ugliness of the merger had put me on the defensive, had taken the steam out of the decision to leave on my own terms.

And now here I was in Ireland, standing beside a ruddy bear of a man whom I'd met only a few hours earlier, considering his invitation to temporarily claim a fragment of this landscape as my own and then open my fingers to let it fall away. I crouched beside the water and sent my little stone tumbling into the stream, taking with it the old ideas about who I was in relation to the work I had been doing. In that liminal moment, I had no clue what I would replace those ideas with, but there they were, washing away toward the Atlantic Ocean, creating a space for something new to begin.

As I stood beside the stream, I gave myself permission to stop trying to be the meaning maker for an organization I no longer recognized or pretended to understand. I not only experienced the release and relief John had intended; I also had a sense of honoring the work I had done in the past by leaving it behind in Ireland, in this place that resonated so deeply with my sense of self. The work that was ahead of me—the work of becoming my own meaning maker—would be harder than what I was leaving behind. I knew that discovering my own voice as a writer would be an important part of this work, and that the sorry excuses for journals I'd been keeping in recent years would not satisfy me once I really got started.

I looked around at people I hardly knew who already had offered me so much comfort, wisdom, and friendship. Compared with the care they were taking with me, I realized how hard I had been on myself in the months leading up to this trip.

The Connemara light shifted again, taking with it the little patch of disappearing landscape from the company I had worked for and in many ways grown up with. My interior geography shifted beside that little stream, too, although it would be a long time before I fully appreciated how profound the shift had been. If someone had told me while I stood there how many times in the years ahead I would conjure that scene in my mind, how much strength I would draw from it, or how fiercely I would hold on to that feeling of letting go, I never would have believed it.

What I knew in the moment was a visceral sense of release—as if I'd been pressing my full weight against a heavy door for a long time, and finally it had burst open. What I understood in the days that followed was that I simply had to give myself over to the magic that was unfolding on that trip. I had to stop standing off to the side. I had to step fully into the picture. And so I did.

I have a hundred happy memories from that once-in-a-lifetime coming together of a community of poets and wanderers who shared a brief stay in the west of Ireland. In our cottages, we brought cups of tea to each other and took turns tending the fires. In pubs, we laughed, tapped our toes, and danced with abandon—yes me, dancing with abandon—to reels and jigs offered up by the locals. In Inishmore, we spread ourselves along the jagged lip of the ancient ruin of Dun Aengus and leaned out to watch waves crash against the cliff a few hundred feet below. Inside a deep green teacup of a sinkhole we draped ourselves across rocks and grass and sat so still one cloudy afternoon that we briefly became part of the landscape—me, still nowhere near a meditative trance, but eyes closed, body at rest. Later we climbed up over the rim of the teacup into dazzling pink clouds just as the sun came out of hiding, setting the bay below us on fire. At David's urging we joined hands and made a long line that rippled along a ridge above the coast, then spiraled into a tight coil, me in one of the inner circles, held up by my friends.

And then it was over, and we scattered back to all the places we had come from.

At home, I let go of parts of my life that no longer fit with who I wanted to be. Three weeks to the day after I dropped my little stone into the stream, it was official: to my great relief, I was not offered the job of managing employee communications in the newly merged company.

I'd like to say that's when I made my great escape from the corporate world. But that's not how it happened. The merger proved to be just a dress rehearsal for my escape, an experience that allowed me to visualize how I would look walking through that heavy door I'd finally pushed open.

I wasn't yet as brave as Jill; I wasn't ready to leave without knowing what I would do next. So with one foot out the door, I lingered at the threshold for a while longer. I accepted a role in the community relations department of the merged company, managing charitable contributions and employee volunteer initiatives. I saw this as a temporary fix—I had no intention of staying. But until I figured out my next move, I'd at least found a safe place to land, and a role that was better suited to the next phase of my journey.

Meanwhile, parts of my interior landscape—the parts I'd been neglecting—continued to shift and began demanding more of my attention. The part of me that used to carry bits of other people's poems around in my head, used to write poems as a way of making sense of the world—she emerged from a long sleep. She even wrote a poem about her recent trip to Ireland, a poem that was published a few months later in a little book of reflections and photographs assembled by the "mystics" as a reminder of the time we'd spent together.

On the desk in my new office I placed the framed photograph of a straggly line of pilgrims in their rain gear in Connemara. Again and again, I allowed myself to be drawn up that hill by my Ballyvaughan friends, beckoned toward a place I still couldn't quite make out through the mist. I couldn't yet see which version of my story was true, which one I needed to tell myself and the people around me. But I knew I could rely on that generous band of seekers to keep lifting me up, and to keep me on a path that would eventually take me where I needed to be.

Happy Groundhog Day

The next ten minutes were a blur. Every time I signed a document and handed it back to Daisy, she passed me a new one, along with another tissue.

After eighteen years in the public affairs department of a large pharmaceutical company, on an otherwise ordinary April afternoon, I let myself out the side door of Corporate America. Then I drove around to the front door, went to the security office, and relinquished a badge that no longer had anything to do with my identity.

"I've heard of you," the woman behind the desk said, as if I were somebody. I would have preferred not to be recognized. I wanted this final transaction to be anonymous. I was leaving by choice and with a sense of great relief. On the inside, I was happier than I'd been in years. But on the outside, my emotions had been spilling over all day, quite unexpectedly.

A routine trip through the breakfast line had set me off for the first time. Two longtime cafeteria employees had greeted me. I wanted to say goodbye but couldn't find my voice.

Then came phone messages from Denise and Alan. Denise was one of the first friends I'd made at the company. We'd stayed in touch after she changed jobs and moved to another city. I had worked for Alan most of the time I'd been there. He'd retired the year before, inadvertently setting off the chain of events that was allowing me to escape. As I listened to those final voicemail messages of my tenure in the corporate world, I teared up again.

I pulled myself together, and two doors down I found my friend Karen. She stepped out from behind her desk to hug me.

"I'm really happy, you know," I managed to squeak out. "But I just got this message from Alan, and one from Denise. I had no idea this would be such an emotional day."

"I'm so happy for you," Karen said. But now she was getting teary too.

We'd been through a lot together. We were both dissatisfied with what the company—and our department—had become. In recent months we'd reminisced about people we'd known, projects we'd worked on, challenges and triumphs, memorable road trips. We'd also reminded each other that the good old days hadn't always been so great. But we knew we'd been part of some important milestones in medicine, in the growth of a small company into a global leader, and in carving out new roles for women in an industry that had long been an old boys' club.

"I just have to get through these next few hours," I said, smiling at the thought. "Then I can go home and finish packing. I'm off to Paris tomorrow to celebrate my great escape."

"Oh, Paree," Karen cooed. "That will make you feel better. Anyway, there's nothing here to be sad about. Anything that was worth crying over ended a long time ago."

I knew she was right. We hugged each other again and I made my way to the ladies room, determined to put my face back together and keep my tears in check.

I appreciated the good wishes from my friends, but they reinforced a feeling I'd had many times in recent months: Most of the people who were familiar with the best work I'd done there were long gone. With few exceptions, those left to bid me goodbye didn't know me well, in part because the company had become so bloated and in part because I'd done my best to fade into the wallpaper. I'd always vowed to leave before I landed on the receiving end of one of those horrible tribute/roast retirement parties. But now that my final day had arrived, it seemed a little pathetic that the closest I would come to an official send-off were two missed phone calls.

I had time to kill until my final appointment with Human Resources. So, for my penultimate act as an employee, I headed to the onsite salon. A manicure relaxed me, and I was amused by the steady stream of people walking in for hair appointments and spa treatments on company time.

While the technician buffed, I remembered a day not long

after I joined the company when I discovered, quite by accident, a barber shop in the basement where busy men (and only busy men) could get their hair trimmed without leaving the building. Now, the dramatically expanded campus offered so many amenities to its thousands of occupants that there was almost no need to go anywhere else for anything else, ever. I understood the on-campus amenities were intended to help with work-life balance. But sometimes it seemed the balance had tipped a little too far, with work being almost an afterthought. Not that I was in a position to judge anyone else's ratio of work to life; after all, soon I would be stepping into unknown territory, my time unstructured and no work to balance with anything else, at least in the short term.

But first I had to let the fresh paint on my fingernails dry, and then I had to keep my last appointment in Human Resources.

Everyone who had been displaced in the Public Affairs reorganization was checking out on the same day, so the HR liaison for the department, Daisy, had a full schedule. The closer it got to my 11:30 appointment, the more confused my emotions became. Signing the final papers—which among other things released the company from legal action regarding my unemployment—was a mere formality, one I'd been itching to execute for more than eight weeks. The waiting period had been designed to assure that any second thoughts were resolved, and to provide a job-search cushion.

I hadn't had so much as the shadow of a doubt since Groundhog Day. As far as I knew, I was the only person leaving of her own free will, invoking a technicality HR most likely had not expected anyone to use. As I pushed the button for the elevator, my stomach started doing little flips. Still, I practically skipped into Daisy's office, knowing the end was in sight.

But by the time she had closed the door behind me, tears were streaming down my face, uncontrollably. Daisy had only been with the company for a few months, and we didn't know each other. I'd met with her briefly when I'd turned in the initial paperwork that confirmed my intention to accept a voluntary separation package. She had no sense of my history there, no knowledge of all I'd been through, no reason to believe me as I sputtered into the tissues she handed me, "Really, I'm not sad about leaving. It's just an emotional day."

The next ten minutes were a blur. Every time I signed a

document and handed it back to Daisy, she passed me a new one, along with another tissue. I was furious with myself for falling apart. In my mind, I had imagined this as a very cool scene, with me being all blasé and Daisy being taken aback by my nonchalance at walking away from a job offer with no new work lined up. In the moment, I blubbered, I dabbed at mascara streaks, I'm sure I left tear stains on some of the papers that secured more than a full year of salary and six months of health care coverage.

I'd long since stopped counting the number of times the public affairs department had been reconfigured, re-engineered, realigned, deconstructed, reconstructed, renamed, or otherwise reinvented since I joined the company in 1987. I'd weathered every storm, moved from one role to the next, been promoted again and again, navigated my way through a de-merger and then a merger. I'd succeeded almost in spite of myself: I'd never been all that ambitious about climbing the corporate ladder or getting a new title. Still, I'd worked my way up from public relations project manager to manager of employee communications to director of community relations.

By the end, even though I'd grown weary of the corporate world and knew I had to escape, I still felt good about the work I was doing in community relations. I was in a field—corporate social responsibility—that was being taken more seriously than in the past. I spent at least as much time working with people outside the company as inside, which made me feel that in some ways I *had* managed to escape, even though I was still there.

As long as they let me keep doing this job, I told myself time and again, *I'll stay. Once they ask me to move on to something else, I'm gone.*

There was no good reason to think I wouldn't be allowed to keep doing that job. Even other public affairs colleagues looked at community relations as being almost beside the point, which was precisely where I wanted to be at that stage in my corporate career.

So late in 2004, when rumors of the latest public affairs "reorg" began to circulate, I assumed it wouldn't have any lasting effect on me. I imagined this exercise would be pretty much the same as all the others: Shave away a little dead wood. Give out some new titles. Shake up the chess pieces and rearrange them on the board, more or less in the same configuration they'd had two reorganizations ago.

Explain that we had to realign to better serve external and internal customers, to create new synergies, to enhance competitiveness, to focus on core competencies, to be sure the right people were in the right jobs at the right time.

Soon, though, it became apparent that this time there would be significant casualties. One autumn afternoon I found myself sitting in an overcrowded, windowless conference room as a senior manager laid out the objectives and timeline for the reorganization. A dozen or so of us were seated around the long table and another ring of chairs was wedged between us and the walls. A few people stood in the corners. The close quarters added to a sense of unease. Some of us did our best to look unconcerned, while others clearly were nervous.

A few slides into her PowerPoint presentation, the manager unveiled terms of separation packages that would be offered to employees who did not find jobs in the soon-to-be streamlined department. Suddenly, the overcrowded room seemed perfect, all that was missing was the music. The rules were being explained for the benefit of those who had not played before, and the fact that separation packages had already been defined made it clear there would not be enough chairs for everyone when the music stopped.

To a casual observer, it may have looked like I had zoned out and was doodling on my notepad; in fact, I was doing the math, multiplying my years of service and my salary by the formula on the slide.

Think of all the time I could buy myself with that kind of a cushion. Time to rethink my goals. Time to make a thoughtful transition to another kind of work, another kind of organization—a transition I've been promising myself for years.

I looked around the room, wondering who was most likely to go away. Unfortunately, it wasn't me. I've never been the kind of employee a manager would opt to get rid of; I work hard, I'm reliable, steady, and eager to please. Really. I had a quarter-century's worth of stellar performance reviews to back me up on this.

So when the first drafts of the new org charts were circulated in November, I mentally penciled my name into two boxes where I thought I might land, both in community relations. Still, I found myself lusting after a separation package, fantasizing about being made redundant. Every job description had been rewritten—if only slightly—so everyone (except the top managers) had to apply for one or more positions and be interviewed as if we were new hires. Many of us were interviewed for two positions at once. This made it impossible to present oneself as preferring either; in my case, it made it easier to be noncommittal.

By December, I had a glimmer of hope. The first round of appointments had been made, and my name had not yet appeared in a box.

On one level, I was insulted—I was more than qualified for both of the positions I'd been interviewed for. I began to wonder if maybe I *had* become the kind of employee a manager wouldn't mind letting go; perhaps my dissatisfaction with myself in that world had become too transparent. On a deeper level, I rejoiced, holding onto the magic PowerPoint formula and the freedom I could almost taste. For once I was paying close attention to the numbers. I knew all the remaining boxes were below—if only slightly—the box I currently occupied. And anything less than a lateral move included the option to take a package.

There was something perverse about wishing so fervently *not* to have a job when the music stopped, surrounded as I was by people who were desperate to stay. But there was also something perverse about the way this reorg was being handled, the murmurings seeping out from beneath constantly closed doors, little clues that implied the process was less about putting the right people in the right jobs, more about cutting costs.

It seemed too good to be true: My years of procrastination and inertia were being rewarded. The exit sign was beckoning. I was nowhere near ready or able to retire at forty-six, but I could see myself taking a few months off, for the one and only time in my adult life. There were, in 2005, plenty of good jobs still to be had. I had no outstanding debt, except for my mortgage, so the short-term financial risk was minimal. The larger risk—the one I was finally embracing—was the emotional one: trying to figure out who I was away from that company, without that ID badge, with no one else left to blame for my work-related unhappiness but me.

As we waited for the next round of interviews, a sort of gallows humor set in. When a coworker (or was it me?) found a headline on the internet that seemed to describe the reorg process, it quickly spread through the ranks: "Massive manure fire burns into third month." Other departments were being streamlined too.

The intranet announced, "Intelligence Affairs function moves to Knowledge Services," but no matter how many times I read the article below that headline, I could not decipher its meaning.

In January, Luanne—a previous manager who'd become a friend—invited me to interview for a role on her new team. The job was an important one—managing communications for the 6,000-person US sales force; it was also a 24/7 commitment, jumping through endless legal and regulatory hoops, and working in the hierarchy-happy sales organization.

I knew I no longer had the stomach for that kind of work. It didn't matter that Luanne was one of the best managers I'd had, or that I liked and respected the vice president of sales, Michael. When Luanne called, I tried to hint at the fact that I didn't want the job.

"Are you telling me you wouldn't accept this job if it was offered?" she asked, a bit testily.

"I don't know what I'm telling you," I replied a bit angrily. "Because I'm not sure what I can or can't say, even to you."

She said I had to be interviewed by Michael, since I couldn't turn down a position that hadn't yet been offered—another rule in the game. So I suffered through the one and only honest conversation I had with anyone in the company during the official proceedings surrounding the reorganization.

Well, Michael was honest anyway.

"Now, Eileen," he said, maintaining steady eye contact as any good salesman would, "We all know what you've done here in the past. I know you've got the skills to handle this position, you're a terrific writer, and you understand all the regulatory challenges around what we do. Luanne is very comfortable working with you and recommending you for this role."

Michael was smart and funny and had a leadership style that set him apart from anyone else I knew in that world. Despite my resolve, I couldn't help but think it would be fun and challenging to work with him.

But Michael wasn't convinced I wanted this job.

"I could be mistaken," he went on, "but it seems to me that since the merger you've almost become invisible. You don't seem to have the same commitment or enthusiasm you had in the past."

I couldn't deny this; more than once we'd both been in

on conversations with other people about the "new" company, conversations that had involved a lot of eye rolling. Now I was being asked to defend myself against charges we both knew were true.

"Well, I think we can agree it's been difficult to adjust to the changes around here."

"Yes, but it's been more than five years since the merger." *Fair point*, I thought.

"We haven't worked together much during that time, and you haven't seen me in action lately," I replied. "I've been a good ambassador for the company in the community. I worked on communications around the headquarters expansion. I helped shape our corporate philanthropy programs, including company giving policies and employee volunteer programs. I've worked hard to help the company develop a solid reputation as a good corporate citizen."

"I don't doubt you've done a good job. But the sales force is the heart of the company. If you're going to work with me, you've got to believe in the company and especially in the sales team. I need to know you will share my belief that we've got the best sales force in the industry. We want them to know they've got the support of the entire organization, and that means giving a 110% effort."

I was impressed with Michael's directness, and I wished I could have returned it in kind and thanked him for calling my bluff. *Sorry, Michael, I'm not your girl*, I wanted to say. But the package, my package, hung in the balance. I couldn't blow the interview by telling him the truth. And I didn't want to embarrass Luanne. I had to make an effort.

"I've been working closely with the regional offices for nearly two years now to develop their local community relations efforts," I reminded him. "If you ask around, I think you'll find I've been a good partner to the sales organization. I've been out in the field, I've volunteered side by side with local teams, and I'm on the phone with managers and reps every day."

It wasn't an answer to his question, but it was all I had.

It went on like that for a few more painful minutes. I fumbled, I fudged. Michael either felt satisfied he'd made his point and wouldn't have to have this conversation with me later if I took the job, or else he simply let me off the hook.

I wouldn't have hired me based on how I handled myself that day. Then again, if it had been up to me, I wouldn't have wasted

Michael's time or mine going through the motions of interviewing for a job I had no intention of accepting. I would have offered me a package back in November, and saved a lot of aggravation all the way around.

When the word came down that those of us who had played through the second round of interviews would learn our fates on February 2, someone (okay, it was me) quickly spread the word that the date had been selected so management could repeat the process over and over until they got it right, just like in the movie *Groundhog Day*.

So late on that early February afternoon, I found myself in a small, sterile conference room, across the table from Luanne. Sun streamed through the windows and reflected off the generic artwork.

"So," she began, "no point keeping you in suspense. I'm glad to offer you the associate director job. Michael likes you, and we know you've got the experience to do this job well. We haven't yet identified the director of employee communications, and you'll be reporting to that person, who will report to me. And of course you'll have a dotted-line relationship to Michael."

I wanted to stop her, wanted to spare us both the details, but she had her spiel prepared and didn't give me an opening. She slipped a sheet of paper out of a leather portfolio and slid it across the table. The page included the new title, salary, and other terms of compensation.

"I know this is an associate director position, and you've been a director." *Uh-oh, here it comes,* I thought. *She's done something to work around the system, and I'm going to be stuck.* But she hadn't, and I wasn't.

"We'll keep your salary at the same level," Luanne continued, "and you really shouldn't think of this as a demotion. It's just that this department is larger and has a different structure."

Up to this point the conversation had gone pretty much as I'd expected. But Luanne closed with a comment I hadn't anticipated: "I want you to know, this is not in any way based on pity. You are totally qualified for this position, and I didn't do anything special to make this happen after you weren't selected for one of the community relations jobs."

"Thanks," I muttered, trying to process that statement, wondering if I had, in fact, become someone Luanne or anyone else might have found worthy of pity. I certainly didn't see myself that way, least of all in this, my singular moment of triumph.

I knew I didn't want and wouldn't accept the job. But I didn't realize until I saw that piece of paper on the table how grateful I was for the offer. That concrete, written offer allowed me to own the decision, to claim my future, instead of being sent away.

"Thanks," I said again, finding my voice while Luanne waited for the response she was sure would follow. "But I'm going to turn down the offer," I said, more steadily than I thought I might. "I want the package. I have to get out of here."

Luanne hadn't mentioned a package, but I knew I had the right to ask for it, according to the rules of the game. It took her a moment to absorb what I'd said. To her credit, she didn't try to change my mind. She asked all the right questions—as a manager and as a friend—to be sure I'd thought through the implications of my decision, including the effects on my pension of leaving before both my twentieth anniversary and my fiftieth birthday. But I'd had months—years, in fact—to contemplate this moment, and I knew without a doubt the decision I'd just announced was the only one I could possibly have made.

Luanne slid the written offer back to her side of the table and tucked it into her folder. She said she would notify Human Resources, then she excused herself so she could let Michael know they needed to find someone else.

And just like that—well, that and the next two months of becoming a little more redundant each day—I went from being part of a well-regarded global organization with tens of thousands of employees to being a one-woman band. It seemed fitting that my midlife experiment officially began on Groundhog Day, when I said "no" to a future shadow of myself I recognized only too well and "yes" to one I couldn't yet begin to perceive.

Famous Pink Raincoat

Despite my fashion faux pas, *that coat suited perfectly my mood on that trip and in that season.*

MARCH IN THE US OF A: EVERY WINDOW I PASSED, EVERY shop where I shopped, pastel-colored spring jackets were on display. On the last business trip of that chapter in my life, I fell for a pink, belted, double-breasted, knee-length raincoat from Jones New York in the crowded racks of Filene's Basement in San Francisco. I folded it into my suitcase for the flight home to Philadelphia, thinking how *au courant* I would look on the vacation I'd planned with my friend Lorraine. I was most emphatically done with my dun-colored, calf-length, practical raincoat.

April in Paris: Lorraine in her tasteful black jacket blended in with natives and tourists alike, all obeying some unwritten rule that permitted only black outerwear. We joked that if we got separated in a crowd, Lorraine would easily find me. Me, in my famous pink raincoat, wandering through the icy drizzle and slick streets of the City of Light, looking like an oversized bottle of Pepto-Bismol, feeling like an experiment with *barbe à papa* (cotton candy) run amok.

And yet: Despite my fashion *faux pas*, that coat suited perfectly my mood on that trip and in that season. I'd just untethered myself from the corporate world with no idea what I'd do next. With my collar turned up against the chill, I wore my heart on a bright pink sleeve, falling in love with the uncertainty of it all. *Ma vie, en rose.*

Birdsong Air • acrylic on canvas

Sifting Through It

Mix dry ingredients in a large bowl and toss with your hands to give the bread a light, airy consistency. Add the softened butter, again with your hands, followed by the raisins.

I've lost track of how many times I've copied over the recipe, double-checking quantities and duplicating the carefully worded instructions from a yellowed index card I keep in a cookie jar with my other favorites. On occasion I've written it down from memory, perhaps forgetting a word here or there, but never failing to include the part about using the hands to give the bread a light, airy consistency, as if omitting those words would somehow slight the memory of Great Aunt Susie, my grandmother's sister, who passed her recipe along to my mother, who passed it along to me.

For years I've been faithfully following this recipe, happily sinking my hands wrist-deep into a floury mess to meld slivers of softened butter—one quarter-pound per loaf—into the dry ingredients. And for years I've shared the recipe with anyone who asks for it, happily inscribing Aunt Susie's name at the top of every index card. In keeping with the spirit of the recipe, I always copy it over by hand, sifting each word through my fingers every time.

And why wouldn't I write "Susie McGuckin's Irish Soda Bread (Scone)" on each copy? My earliest recollections of eating the bread are at Aunt Susie's dining room table—sometimes after a meal, sometimes just as the centerpiece of an evening visit. Social calls from one house to another for no particular occasion were a high form of entertainment during the 1960s, at least in my family. An announced visit to see Aunt Susie and Uncle Hughie was a treat any day of the week, and the sooner you knew you were going, the more time you had to anticipate it.

Aunt Susie always met us at the front door of their tidy stone twin, as if she'd been looking forward to the visit as much as we had. She was a great hugger, and she held on long enough to let you know she meant it. Uncle Hughie hovered nearby, waving everyone into the living room and waiting until we were all settled on the sofa, chairs, or bottom steps before he re-installed himself in his recliner, happy for a diversion from his newspaper.

A visit always began in the living room with polite conversation among the adults and a chance to catch up on local and long-distance family news. Aunt Susie offered compliments on the good manners of her great nieces and nephews (which tended to be better in her living room than they were in our own). She dandled the littlest baby on her lap and cooed over how much he'd grown in such a short time. And then, as we knew she would, she dashed off to the kitchen and set the kettle to boil.

We never lingered long in Aunt Susie's living room because it was obvious from the moment we walked in the door that we were destined to wind up in the adjacent dining room, which had all the trappings of an elegant tea party on full display. In my mind I see a crisp white tablecloth covered with delicate plates and a matching teapot in a quilted cozy. I hear the gentle clink-clink of spoons in teacups and see a cut-glass butter dish and a shallow bowl filled with orange marmalade being passed up one side of the table and down the other. Each slab of soda bread would have been generously slathered with both toppings, then washed down with tea.

Aunt Susie made me and my younger sister Angie feel grown up by pouring tea for us at her well-dressed table, while our little brothers got milk or maybe ginger ale. The tea was black and bitter to begin with, although for a young guest it was laced with so much milk and sugar that its color was nearly indistinguishable from the pearly inside of the cup it came in.

Even though Aunt Susie had prettily arranged packaged cookies on a plate and let us help ourselves to them, she'd serve Angie and me each a slice of soda bread, as if that somehow elevated our status at her table. Aunt Susie would clap her hands together and laugh out loud at my childish habit of meticulously picking every raisin out of the bread (a habit that persisted well into adulthood). She never minded that I left a small brown pile of uneaten fruit at the edge of my plate. But she never left out the raisins, either.

Sometimes one of Aunt Susie's tea parties would end with me and Angie staying over for a few happy days. We were lucky enough to fit perfectly into the space between Aunt Susie's emptying nest and the arrival of her own grandchildren. She made such a fuss over us—in all the best ways—and loved showing us off to her neighbors. Not once during one of these visits did an ice cream truck pass Aunt Susie's thick hedge of hydrangeas (Angie and I still call them "Aunt Susie flowers") without Uncle Hughie or our teen-aged cousin Mary Ann being dispatched to the curb on our behalf.

Beat the eggs. Add the buttermilk and blend. Make a well in the dry ingredients and pour the egg mixture slowly into the center. Blend well with a spoon.

I don't remember ever watching Aunt Susie make her soda bread, although I spent plenty of time in her kitchen. In fact, I don't remember her cooking much of anything, although I am certain I never once went home hungry from her house.

I loved the cabinet where she kept her spices, as well as staples like baking powder and baking soda, both of which are called for in the recipe. Behind a door under the kitchen counter was a round, multi-tiered revolving shelf loaded with tins and jars. I loved to spin the shelf so the shapes and scents of the containers blurred, sometimes making me sneeze. Aunt Susie never stopped me from playing this game, even when I got to be tall enough that I had to crouch low beside the shelf to spin it, using the pretext of amusing a younger sibling. Every other spice cabinet I've since happened upon (or stocked) has reminded me of Aunt Susie's kitchen.

I do remember watching my mother make soda bread, almost always for special occasions like Saint Patrick's Day or Christmas. Year after year, she sent my father off to work with freshly baked loaves for each of those holidays. Sometimes she sent us to school with holiday loaves for our teachers. After the bread cooled on wire racks, Mom always wrapped it tightly in tin foil and sometimes stuck a bow on top or tied a ribbon around a finished loaf to complete the packaging.

After college, I began my own tradition of baking soda bread for coworkers, and I've hardly missed a St. Patrick's Day or a Christmas in nearly four decades. Aunt Susie's recipe doesn't say anything about wrapping the bread in tin foil, but it's the only thing I know to do with the loaves once I've baked them. I imagine in the rural Ireland of Aunt Susie's early years they would have used a linen tea towel. I think of the foil as an American ingredient we've folded into the old tradition.

My parents both are first-generation Irish-Americans. I've always understood making soda bread for the outside world to be a way of celebrating our Irishness, of sharing it with other people. Still, when I was growing up, except for those two times of the year, soda bread usually only appeared in our house when Irish relatives visited or, as I noticed over time, when someone died and one of us kids would be sent to the grocery store for buttermilk and raisins so a loaf could be baked and delivered to the bereaved household, a kind of comfort food.

We never called it soda bread back then; we only ever called it "scone"—a word that rhymed with "gone," not "stone," although a loaf is as dense and as heavy as a river rock. I still don't understand why it would be called soda bread. The recipe calls for only one-quarter teaspoon of baking soda, the smallest quantity of any of the nine ingredients.

My mother didn't sift the dry ingredients with her hands. She scooped flour into a rickety aluminum sifter, then squeezed the looped handle to scrape a thin metal wheel across a mesh surface. I never could see much difference between what was spooned into the sifter from above and what snowed into the waiting bowl below. I took it on faith that this step mattered. Later, I came to see the mechanical sifter as my mother's more modern way of achieving the light, airy consistency mentioned in Aunt Susie's recipe.

I remember a feeling of ritual about watching my mother make soda bread as a child and a thrill of excitement at being old enough to help grease and flour the pans, measure out ingredients, or sift the flour. I remember the warm, doughy smell that spread through the house as the loaves began to rise. I remember looking for golden-brown bits of the crusty top I could break off and eat without getting caught. And I remember watching my mother's father pour leftover buttermilk into a jelly glass and drink the thick, tangy liquid down in one gulp. As a child, it made me shudder to think of drinking buttermilk, even if it did somehow taste like Ireland to him.

When I went to Ireland for the first time in my thirties, I was so used to Aunt Susie's scone recipe that I had a hard time swallowing—literally—the dry little cakes that went by the same name there. I've been back several times since, and I have yet to see a loaf of homemade soda bread in any of the dozen or more family homes I've had the pleasure of visiting, including the one where my grandmother and Aunt Susie grew up. I can't get enough of the ubiquitous brown bread in Ireland, baked fresh or fetched from the grocery in a plastic bag. But I never have warmed up to the soda bread there. Even with butter, it's dry and disappointing.

Perhaps it only tastes so good *here* because it evokes *there*. Or maybe they're just skimping on the buttermilk.

The dough should be heavy, but not too wet. If it seems too dry, add more buttermilk.

It always seems too dry, so I always add more buttermilk. And I always make two scones at a time because you can't buy less than a quart of buttermilk, and what else can you do with it once you've opened the carton? Following Aunt Susie's recipe, I use my hands to sift the dry ingredients together and then to work the butter (already sliced in small bits) into the flour mixture. In fact, a small confession—much smaller than the one I'm working up to—I also use my hands to work the wet ingredients into the dry ones, a sticky but satisfying step I invented myself.

While I'm at it, one more small confession: these days I leave an ounce or two of buttermilk in the carton so I can savor it after I've placed the dough-laden pans in the oven. My grandfather would have loved to catch me at that.

Only once in my whole history of knowing Aunt Susie could the words "heavy" and "wet" have been used to describe her. I was not quite ten when Uncle Hughie died—suddenly, of a heart attack, not long after he'd retired. I remember leaving the funeral home after the viewing, walking through the parking lot with my parents and Aunt Susie. She walked slowly, maybe even a little unsteadily, and she leaned hard on my shoulder, her face still wet with tears. I felt such an odd blend of emotions—sad for the heaviness of her sorrow, grateful for the opportunity to do something for her, completely at a loss for what to say at such a grown-up moment.

Of course Aunt Susie had known other sorrows, too, but those I was too young to comprehend at the time. Only later did I begin to understand how much the loss of a sister would have weighed on her middle years, how heavy her heart would have been during the time she was such a happy presence in my childhood. And only now in my own middle age do I fully appreciate how much of herself Aunt Susie poured into the hollow well of her sister's family, as if she had all the buttermilk in the world to spare.

It's no wonder she was an honored guest at every birthday, every christening, every first communion, every graduation, every wedding, every special occasion for our extended family for as long as she lived—nearly eighty-five years. It's no wonder I cooked up my own tradition of having tea parties with my nieces and nephews when they were little and came to visit me, even if I sometimes substituted fruity herbal teas or juice for the real thing in my teapot and made waffles the signature treat at my dining room table. And it's no wonder I still use soda bread as an excuse to invoke Aunt Susie's name, to hold onto a little slice of her. Sometimes I even bake a couple random loaves between St. Patrick's Day and Christmas, for a birthday party or a brunch.

"Your soda bread was especially good today," my mother noted at the end of a family gathering at my house as I wrapped a slab of it in foil for her to take home. We've broken so many loaves together over the years that the bread itself is rarely discussed, although the gesture of baking it is always appreciated. So I was surprised Mom thought my latest loaf was worth mentioning. I figured she was just reacting to how moist it was.

"I have a heavy hand with the buttermilk," I confessed, thinking that would explain why this batch of bread tasted especially good. The amount of buttermilk was, after all, the only variable allowed for in the family recipe.

"What recipe are you using?" she persisted.

"Aunt Susie's recipe, of course. It's the only soda bread recipe I've ever used."

I pulled out the worn index card to show her. She knew at a glance it wasn't the recipe she knew by heart.

"That's definitely not Aunt Susie's recipe. It's good, though."

The party was over and Mom was halfway out the door, Dad already waiting in the car, so she didn't tell me how she knew my recipe wasn't Aunt Susie's. I had to admit the chances of Mom being in possession of the real recipe were better than good—she was, after all, a generation closer to the source. Also, upon careful inspection, I could see how I had penciled in the words "Susie McGuckin's" above my original black-ink heading, "Irish Soda Bread (Scone)." But how different could the recipes be? What's half a cup of buttermilk among family?

Still, I began to wonder where *my* recipe had come from and when I had started attributing it to Aunt Susie. Was it around the time of her death, now more than thirty years ago? And was that also when I'd begun to substitute plump golden raisins for the brown ones I so despised? Or was it later, perhaps out of guilt, when I started to omit the raisins altogether and began to experiment with cranberry scones at Christmastime and chocolate chip scones in other seasons? I remember Mom suggesting I may have strayed too far from the Irish tradition with the chocolate chips, although she didn't object to how it tasted; and she was the first one of us to substitute cranberries for raisins.

One day at my parents' house, shortly after I discovered I'd been passing off someone else's recipe as Aunt Susie's, I pulled out Mom's recipe box to compare the true version with mine. I discovered a whole collection of soda bread recipes in that box, one of which was attributed to Aunt Susie. As I scanned the list of ingredients and jotted them onto a scrap of paper, I could see obvious differences from the recipe I used.

Later, when I put the two lists side by side on my kitchen counter, I could hardly believe my eyes: Except for four cups of flour and two eggs, our other ingredients didn't match at all. Mom's version of Aunt Susie's recipe doesn't even call for those offensive raisins, which I have dutifully included in every copy I've ever handed out, despite my own deep reservations.

Where my recipe calls for half a cup of sugar, Aunt Susie's calls for a full cup. Where mine calls for a cup-and-a-half of buttermilk (for starters), Aunt Susie's calls for half a cup of buttermilk and half a cup of whole milk. Aunt Susie used four teaspoons of baking powder to my two, and no salt compared with my half-teaspoon.

And get this: My measly quarter-teaspoon of baking soda is a quarter-teaspoon more than Aunt's Susie's recipe calls for. That's right, her *soda bread* did not contain even a trace of baking soda.

The biggest discrepancy, though, is also the biggest surprise: Susan Donnelly McGuckin, born and bred in butter-loving Ireland, used not so much as a dollop of the artery-clogging substance to make her scone. Her American-born, generally health-conscious great-niece has for decades been making soda bread with a stick of butter in every loaf, in deference to her Irish roots and the great esteem in which she holds the memory of her great aunt. And she's passed off this buttery impersonation as the real deal to scores of unsuspecting Americans who obviously don't know any better.

This also means my mother, who fondly recalls being discovered at a tender age sitting under her mother's kitchen table eating butter—just butter—with her fingers, has never baked butter into her soda bread. Although, as previously noted, the slathering of butter onto the baked bread has always been encouraged in our family.

Furthermore, Aunt Susie's recipe is no more than a list of ingredients, carefully transcribed in my mother's neat handwriting, with the only instruction being to bake the bread at 350° for 45 minutes. No advice about using one's hands, making a well in the dry ingredients, or sensing the subtle distinction between "heavy" and "too wet."

In hindsight, I'm sure Aunt Susie would have thought any self-respecting baker who had that list of ingredients handed to her ought to already know to mix the wet and dry ingredients separately, then introduce them to each other in some appropriate way.

When I stopped to think about it, I realized Aunt Susie probably didn't even use a recipe. She just had a feel for how much of this and how much of that to toss into a bowl. The recipe in my mother's box might be no more than a list of ingredients Aunt Susie rattled off on the phone for her one day.

"Now let's see," she began as she twisted the cord on the heavy black phone that sat on a small table in the corner of her dining room. "You start with four cups of flour. And about a cup of sugar..." If the phone had been in the kitchen, she could have opened her spice rack and spun it around to remind herself of the ingredients. Maybe she simply forgot to mention the baking soda. And perhaps the butter too.

Clearly my recipe is not the family heirloom I've always thought it to be. Although to be honest it has every advantage over Aunt Susie's recipe in producing a moist, buttery scone. No wonder my grandfather wound up with a full glass of buttermilk every time my mother baked scones. No wonder I learned from an early age that soda bread is always served with gobs of butter (Aunt Susie would have said "buther") and marmalade.

Dust hands with flour and mold dough into a round. Place into a greased 9" pan and dust the top generously with flour.

How many times have I copied those words without once picking up on the obvious clue that this could not have been Aunt Susie's recipe? A "round"? We've always made our soda bread in loaf pans, not rounds. I always make a parenthetical note on the copies I give out indicating I prefer a loaf pan; but Aunt Susie's real recipe never would have required such an annotation.

Once I had this small epiphany, others followed. For example: In the first thirty years of my life, when I frequently had the pleasure of spending time with Aunt Susie, I never heard her utter a phrase even half as pretentious as "light, airy consistency." It would be fair to say she herself had a light, airy consistency; and a soft, powdery cheek; and a voice that was equal parts whistle and lilt, wrapped up in a Northern Irish brogue-burr.

Aunt Susie could comfort you and laugh at you at the same time, although you never felt she was laughing at you, just that she was lightening the mood, helping you see how small your little crisis was.

And I'm sure that if she did dust her soda bread with flour, she would have done so generously, because generous was the essence of Aunt Susie.

The soda bread I bake with a generous quarter-pound of butter in every loaf must taste different from the version Aunt Susie made and my mother learned to imitate. But I can't say I ever really noticed the difference while I was eating it. Maybe their butterless bread was no better than the disappointing little tea cakes I've sampled in Ireland.

I mean if you take away the raisins, which I always did, what was left for a child to find appealing in a slice of that bread? A trace of fruity residue in the spots I'd plucked the raisins from and a slight tang imparted by the buttermilk. But otherwise, a dry loaf that had no business masquerading as a dessert and should have sent me reaching for the cookie plate every time. But it didn't.

Perhaps all along I've been savoring the butter and the marmalade, not giving proper attention to the bread below. I'm not sure the syrupy suspension that holds the marmalade together, undercut by the bitterness that lingers in the strips of orange rind, would have appealed to me as a child. I wasn't the most adventurous eater, so it seems unlikely my palate would have been charmed by such complexity. A more likely explanation is that I perceived my willingness to eat soda bread and marmalade as a measure of my worthiness to drink tea with the grownups. Or even more importantly, I saw it as a way to demonstrate to them that I took my Irishness—and theirs—seriously.

And what could be more Irish than the layer of sweet cream butter that lurked beneath the marmalade? Butter that had been taken out of the fridge far enough in advance to be spreadable, but was still cool enough that it didn't melt until it landed on my tongue. The pleasure of this buttery sensation surely would have compensated for a lack of shortening in the bread itself and just might have overridden the encounter between my young taste buds and the bittersweet marmalade.

If she *had* put butter in her soda bread, I like to think Aunt Susie would have used her hands for the task, like I do. Aunt Susie's hands were always busy. She knew how to brush her fingers across your cheek or squeeze your arm in just the right way, at just the right time. She could deftly gauge your length and your width using a measuring tape and, in an afternoon, whip up matching dresses for you and your sister on her dining room table without a pattern. In rare idle moments, Aunt Susie's long, thin fingers would flit around her gray hair, poking at stray bobby pins, then settle nervously in her lap.

Maybe I let myself believe I was using Aunt Susie's recipe because it was easy to picture her pushing up her sleeves and working her hands into that wet-heavy-sticky dough, which come to think of it, produces a bread that is neither light nor airy.

Using the wrong end of a fork, cut a deep cross into the dough to prevent the top from cracking and to give the bread a traditional look.

Bake at 350° one hour or until well browned.

Good, practical advice, that part about the fork. It almost sounds like something Aunt Susie might have said, although I'm not sure she would have mixed baking advice with religion, even though the towering stone church she attended for years sat just across the driveway from her kitchen window.

After I compared my recipe with Mom's, I called to be sure I hadn't simply forgotten to copy butter from her list of ingredients.

"There's no butter in it," Mom confirmed. "That's why we always serve it on the side."

"Well, my recipe calls for a quarter pound of butter," I admitted, "and I still serve it on the side."

I also explained that my recipe had three times as much buttermilk, but she dismissed that: "I always add extra buttermilk," she admitted, "and I never use a whole cup of sugar, maybe half a cup at most."

We laughed to think we'd both been giving out different recipes in Aunt Susie's name, even though my version isn't even close; Mom improvises liberally with hers; and we both sometimes substitute other ingredients for the raisins Aunt Susie failed to mention, although she certainly used them. We agreed Aunt Susie would toss back her head and have a good, long laugh with us—and maybe a little bit at us—if she knew what had become of her recipe in our hands.

I don't think she would have minded the substitutions, though. Aunt Susie knew a thing or two about making due with the ingredients at hand. And while she never would have pretended to be a substitute for her missing sister, she managed to improvise the roles of "aunt" and "great aunt" until they took on a flavor that was uniquely hers.

Of course people were eating soda bread in Ireland long before they had the luxury of ovens that could be calibrated to 350°. I've seen recipes that call for cooking scone in an iron skillet over an open flame. In fact, I used to have a recipe just like that, printed on an oversized Irish linen tea towel, which hung on the butter-yellow kitchen wall of my first apartment. The illustration that accompanied the recipe showed a skillet with a round, brown loaf being tended by a white-bearded leprechaun—just the sort to cook up a batch of blarney about a two-pound loaf of bread with a light, airy consistency.

I've long since lost track of that tea towel.

But I suspect, now that I know where my soda bread recipe *didn't* come from, that woven into the threads of that Irish linen was a list of nine ingredients, two of which were a cup-and-a-half of buttermilk and a quarter-pound of butter, all of which I just may have copied onto an index card, along with some overly fancy language about how to assemble those ingredients.

What's funny is that regardless of the recipes we start with, most of the time the soda bread we bake in my family winds up tasting more or less the same; that is, it tastes like a tradition that's been handed down from one country to another, one generation to the next, one oven, one loaf pan, one index card at a time. Any way you sift it, any way you slice it, each loaf is a reminder of good old Irish hospitality at good old Great Aunt Susie's dining room table, "buther" or not.

Interior Spaces

> *Once I'd begun, it was like pulling at a loose thread on a sweater—the entire room began to unravel. Empty, the shelves sagged and tilted. Exposed, the plaster walls had hairline fractures and deep gouges.*

Bang. Bang, bang, bang.

Another shelf pried loose.

Bang, bang, bang, bang.

Nails bent and hammered into the wood. Another careful trip around the narrow landing, down the stairs, through the front door, down the driveway. Another long plank deposited beside the telephone pole. Back up the stairs.

Bang, bang, bang.

It felt good to be swinging a hammer, good to be working my body, giving my mind a rest. I felt busy, productive. And oddly satisfied to be breaking things down, splintering wood, and dismantling the dark-stained desk, the uneven shelves, the flimsy cabinets. Out with the old.

I knew my next-door neighbors would be curious about the growing heap of lumber near the curb. Good. Maybe that would keep long-retired, well-intentioned George from asking about my job search or commenting on how much I seemed to enjoy spending time on my front porch.

A few months earlier, I'd given myself permission to take the summer off after leaving a company where I'd worked for eighteen years. I knew I had to get serious about finding a new job. But first, I had to face up to the 11x14-foot disaster area that was my home office. I'd intended to remodel that room when I'd moved in four years earlier, but somehow the project never made it to the top of my home improvement list. Now, before I pushed myself back out into the world, I had to take that room apart and put it back together again. At the outset, I didn't appreciate how much the room makeover had to do with the process of reinventing myself and—at long last—carving out the space for my writing life to begin in earnest. And not just the physical space.

When I'd first seen the house, I'd fallen for the built-in bookshelves in the living room. A ready-made office in one of the four small bedrooms—with a built-in desk in one corner and floor-to-ceiling shelves on three walls—seemed too good to be true. But now, lopsided stacks of books, boxes of photographs, and seemingly every scrap of paper I'd amassed in nearly half a century of living had overtaken the office.

I'd started clearing out the room in July, when it was too hot for the demolition work. I'd dragged countless boxes and bags across the small upstairs hallway, covering virtually every inch of available floor space in two other rooms.

In July, I still half-believed I could salvage the built-ins with a fresh coat of paint, maybe some new trim. I soon discovered that like every other project in my 1923-vintage house, there were no quick fixes. Once I'd begun, it was like pulling at a loose thread on a sweater—the entire room began to unravel. Empty, the shelves sagged and tilted. Exposed, the plaster walls had hairline fractures and deep gouges. And cleared of debris, the homemade desk from another era was an ergonomic nightmare for a computer.

And that's just what was going on in the room; in my head, things were tilting and unraveling, too, exposing damaged surfaces and occasionally giving me nightmares.

By August, it was clear I'd have to demolish the built-ins and invest in new furniture.

By September, renovating the room—as exhausting as it was physically—had become the easy part of the project.

Bang.

Bang, bang, bang.

It had been a long, hot summer, as evidenced by my sweat-soaked clothes, my damp hair, and the blazing sun that beat down on my freckled arms with every trip I made down the driveway with an armful of broken-up furniture.

All summer I'd been working out in my head—or trying to—who I wanted to be at the end of my midlife respite from work. I'd been reading books and attending "outplacement" classes funded by my former employer. I was almost certain I wanted to find my next job in the nonprofit sector, although I hadn't entirely ruled out starting a freelance writing business. I had a pretty good idea of what I didn't want to do next—virtually anything I had done up to that point. In August, I attended a nonfiction writing conference, although I felt like an impostor identifying myself as an actual writer; never mind that my summer of discontent had been punctuated with happy fits of writing, and I knew whatever I did next would have to allow for that to continue.

Still, I had more questions than answers about what my next chapter would look like. Until that September, it never occurred to me that some of the answers might be hiding under all that clutter from my office, or what I'd come to think of as the Museum of Me.

I dismantled the built-ins little by little. Early on each of my demolition mornings, before it got too hot in my un-air-conditioned house, I'd start with quiet tasks. I'd unscrew hinges or use a crowbar to coax strips of lumber and particleboard away from the floor and the interior walls of the cabinets below the desk. I'd tape paint swatches to the yellowed walls or browse online for new, functional furniture. Then, once it was a respectable hour to start making noise, I'd let the hammer ring out against the wood, working as long as I could.

Then I'd shower, slip into clean shorts and a fresh t-shirt, and grab a pile of artifacts from one of the other rooms. I'd plunk myself down on the bare hardwood floor in the middle of the mess I was both making and unmaking. I'd wedge open a dusty box, a creaky binder, or a long-forgotten journal, and there I'd stay for an hour, maybe three, right in the middle of some earlier version of myself.

Sometimes I felt guilty about all the time I was spending sorting through my archives. I should be writing, I'd think as I flipped through speeches I'd written for other people, pictures of long-lost friends, copies of invoices from my days as a freelance medical editor. I should be looking for a job, I'd worry as I sifted through airline ticket stubs, old performance reviews, or notes a younger me had made in the margins of her books. I should be getting out of the house more, I'd chide myself as I reread papers I'd written in graduate school, flipped through postcards I'd collected while traveling, thumbed through the high school and college yearbooks I'd helped to edit.

Yet day after day I stayed there, deciding what to keep, what to toss, what to shred; sometimes the shredding was practical (old pay stubs), other times cathartic (old boyfriends). Some items I kept to remind me of who or where I didn't want to be anymore—a box of crayons from an absurd management meeting near the end of my corporate tenure. Some I saved because they made me laugh—a photograph of me and two coworkers in our 1980s business attire on roller skates (it's a long story); or because they made me cry—letters, obituaries cut from the newspaper; or because they helped me remember who I'd been—old business cards; or who I'd meant to be—scraps of poems I'd started, newsletter articles I'd written, words that had my name attached to them.

Bang.

Bang, bang, bang.

All those exposed surfaces to spackle and sand. All the possibilities contained in a can of paint. All the October days spent dragging newly delivered furniture pieces up the stairs and around the narrow landing to make a new desk, new bookshelves, new file cabinets. Some assembly required. All the nails driven into four freshly painted walls to hang photographs and artwork carefully curated from my collections—or purchased for my new space—to surround me, remind me, inspire me. All the talismans artfully arranged to keep me true to myself until I found my way back into the world again; and again, after that.

If anyone had asked about all the hammering—say my neighbor George—I would have said I was up to my eyeballs in yet another home improvement project. Only I knew what had really been going on up there, under all that paper, over all that splintered wood and plaster dust.

Enchanted Places • acrylic and collage on board

Santa Fe Stories

> *After a quarter century of being a business traveler, I was a free agent, laptopless and without the benefit—or burden—of business cards. How would this new, evolving me play in Santa Fe?*

I WENT TO SANTA FE WITH A SUITCASE FULL OF STORIES, my own in-progress writings, and every good intention of spending evenings in my tiny casita, reading and writing, editing and honing. Taking my stories along had helped justify my retreat into the desert and away from the circle of family and friends whose once-staunch support for my midlife experiment had begun to wane. I was tired of explaining my decision to take a sabbatical after leaving a company where I'd worked for nearly two decades. Even worse, I had begun to grow weary of the sabbatical itself. Not going to work every day had become its own rut, and my middle-class guilt was gaining on me.

I'd been half-heartedly looking for a job for months. But I still couldn't figure out what kind of work I wanted to do. I was much better at articulating what I didn't want to do—more of the same, corporate communications. I'd come to think of all the years I'd spent in that field as time I'd given over to other people's stories. I needed to find a way into my own next chapter. I'd been writing in earnest for all those months when it looked to everyone else like I wasn't working; only I knew how much work was involved in discovering my own, true stories.

Sixteen months earlier, I'd opted for a "separation package" and walked away from a job I knew I didn't want. Initially, I'd only planned to take a few months off; after more than thirty years of steady employment and with that package in my pocket, why not? But a few months had turned into half a year, then a whole year, and now even I was beginning to wonder if I was ever going to find a job that felt like the right next move.

How could I dare to take so much time out of the workforce? On top of that, I needed a vacation? "From what?" I could hear the chorus asking, my own voice louder than any other.

I wasn't sure I believed my own story anymore.

I went to Santa Fe to keep a promise too. In the early days of being unemployed, I'd made a lot of lists: groceries to buy, people to call, books to read, movies to see, places to volunteer, home improvement projects to tackle. Lists helped to structure my suddenly unspoken-for time. Sometimes I added a task to a list after I'd already done it, just for the satisfaction of crossing it off. Near the top of my list of "big" things to do between jobs, I had scrawled: *Santa Fe – at last, and at least.*

I arrived in Santa Fe on a weekday afternoon, following a long day of travel from Pennsylvania. I checked into a hotel several blocks west of the historic Plaza and set off on foot to get my first look at "The City Different." After months of geographical inertia, it was a thrill to be somewhere new, free to slip in and out of museums, coffee shops, galleries, restaurants—anywhere—unknowing and unknown.

I had the town to myself, at least for the first ten minutes or so of my stroll. On West San Francisco Street, shops and galleries were closed, sidewalks were empty, restaurants were not yet open for dinner. Even the stately El Dorado Hotel seemed to be at rest. I half-expected a tumbleweed to blow by. The low-slung adobe buildings, many housing high-end artwork and clothing boutiques, initially struck me as a cross between Rodeo Drive and the Wild West. Filling the horizon at the far end of San Francisco Street was St. Francis Cathedral, its pale facade honey-drizzled in the late-day sun.

I paused to admire the ornate details of the Lensic, an old theater just two blocks off the Plaza, not yet realizing what the former vaudeville house held in store for me. Then I noticed the posters. I'd arrived just in time for the second annual Santa Fe Short Story Festival, several days of dramatic readings featuring local storytellers and an impressive cast of actors. The box office had just closed, so I started a to-do list for the next day: *Tix for short story festival.*

From a distance, Santa Fe had seemed to offer an opportunity to lose myself in an unknown city, to quietly find that clear sense of self that bubbles to the surface when I travel, especially when I travel alone. But as I quickly discovered, Santa Fe does not encourage visitors to be there in a quiet way; Santa Feans draw you out and ask you where you're from, why you're there, what *your* story is. They want to tell their stories too—how they came for the mountains, the art, or the desert, and then decided to stay. Before my first lunch in Santa Fe, I was lost in a swirl of stories, a barrage of biographical data, much of it unsolicited. And all I'd done was take a walking tour, wander into a few downtown galleries, and drift into a bookstore.

I hadn't yet decided which story I wanted to tell the friendly strangers in this town. I'd come to see myself as being not just between jobs but also between identities, between versions of myself. After a quarter century of being a business traveler, I was a free agent, laptopless and without the benefit—or burden—of business cards. How would this new, evolving me play in Santa Fe? How would I present myself in a place where no one knew my story? Did I dare introduce myself as a writer? I had, after all, hauled a few pounds of paper across the country as proof of my commitment to my craft. If anyone asked what I had to show for all those months of being unemployed, surely writing would count for something. Still, in Santa Fe I was surrounded by people who'd given themselves over entirely to their art. I hadn't gone nearly that far, and I wasn't sure I was ready to present myself as an artist in such an art-full place. I was as much a work in progress as the stories at the bottom of my suitcase.

The first night of the Short Story Festival featured master storytellers from the pueblos of New Mexico—ancient, mostly soft-spoken American Indians, their faces mirroring the colors and folds of the Sangre de Cristo Mountains that formed the backdrop for the event, held outdoors at the Institute of American Indian Arts. These elders shared stories from their own lives and stories that had been handed down to them, sometimes weaving both together. A fragile woman with a stiff, heavy blanket over her shoulders recounted how as a child she'd spotted "Mother Salt" in a peanut butter jar in her grandmother's cupboard—a parable about the importance of salt to her ancestors even as modern ways seeped into the pueblos. A tall, broad man with a quavering voice told of a young boy who'd set off in search of his missing brother; the tale twisted, turned magical, and then trailed off as the storyteller strained to compete with rumbling thunder in the mountains and grumbling motorcycles in the Plaza. A woman with a steady, lilting voice conjured three sisters, two who primped and preened to impress the boys in their village, while a third stayed home to tend the fire and take care of other chores; this story seemed vaguely familiar.

The thread that wove these tales together was soaring, haunting music by Red Skyhawk, played on a Native flute at the beginning and end of each storyteller's performance. He was a generation or two removed from the elders, but like them he wore traditional clothes. He took great care in guiding each storyteller onto the stage. His music, like their stories, was offered as a gift to the audience. The storm, which felt imminent throughout the evening, stayed in the distance, where sheets of rain could be seen through a dazzling sunset.

I was hooked; Santa Fe had stories to tell, and I was there to listen.

And so my brief sojourn in Santa Fe unfolded—with museums, shops, and galleries by day, and stories every night. The only evening I'd planned in advance was a trip to the Santa Fe Opera for a production of Massenet's *Cendrillon (Cinderella)*. I thought I knew this story; in fact I'd heard echoes of it in the Native tale of the three sisters. But I didn't know until I read the program that more than a thousand variations of the Cinderella story have been found, dating back to ninth-century China and spanning world cultures. I'd grown up with the Rodgers & Hammerstein made-for-television musical without knowing children in other places knew darker versions like "Aschenputtel" by the Brothers Grimm, in which the mean stepsisters have their eyes pecked out by birds.

Not for the first time, I wondered how many versions of *my* story could be told. Surely not a thousand. But so many more than one true story, depending on which scenes were selected, which traits and supporting characters were emphasized, and of course, who was telling the story and to whom it was being told. And that was just if I looked backward; looking ahead, who knew what might transpire? Which new characters or events would lead me to reinterpret or discard others I'd already made sense of or had come to see as essential? Which threads from the past would the future pull at, which new textures would be woven into my story over time?

Cendrillon was sumptuous. A set framed by walls covered with text from the libretto—French words writ large in black on white as if a calligrapher had gone mad. An over-the-top fairy godmother. Improbably geometric, bright-red ball gowns for the stepsisters and other princess-wannabes. Cendrillon's gown glimmered with crystal beads, a hint of ash near the hem so subtle I might have imagined it. From beneath the roof of the open amphitheater, dramatic flashes of lightning backlit the mountains, but for the second straight night, the sky spared both storytellers and audience.

The next evening I rejoined the Short Story Festival at the Lensic. Actors, many with New Mexico connections, read stories they had chosen. Alan Arkin opted for truth over fiction; his emotional reading of a letter sent by Hermann Hesse to a German government minister in 1917, "If the War Goes on Another Two Years...," left many in the audience saddened by a slice of history repeating, but now in the Middle East and Afghanistan. On the following evening, the festival closed with dramatic readings of two classic stories—an Oscar Wilde and a Raymond Chandler—brought to life by a cast that included Ali McGraw, Judge Reinhold, and Shirley MacLaine, to the delight of a packed theater.

As the festival ended, I realized I'd whiled away my Santa Fe evenings with other people's stories, not my own. I felt surprisingly guilt-free about this. There were stories in the air in this place, and without even trying I'd been making connections between the undisturbed pages back in my casita and the stories I'd been offered in Santa Fe.

It occurred to me that perhaps it had been more important to get out of my own head than it had been to get out of my house.

Everywhere I went first-person narratives, impromptu conversations, spontaneous confessions, and mid-life conversions found me in Santa Fe. At first they caught me by surprise, but soon I learned to listen, to let stories wash over me like the clouds and light that shifted overhead from dawn until dusk in the wide

New Mexico sky. The couple who said they'd come for a visit, taken one lap around the Plaza, and knew they were "home." The potter who'd moved from New Jersey and was never going back. The woman who'd abandoned New York to run a day spa. New beginnings, all. Fresh chapters in their stories. If they could do it, I could, right?

I met people who'd gone off script, abandoned other careers, other places, other people's expectations. They were hard at work rewriting themselves out here in the desert, in the shadows of sepia-tinged mountains. And they were just as interested in hearing my story as they were in telling me theirs. I discovered I was in a place that offered many ways into another person's story; and not once did I hear the one I knew best and was least comfortable with: "What do you do for a living?"

At times it seemed I was having one big, long conversation with Santa Fe—and she was a sparkling conversationalist. She knew just what to tell me, and she had a way about her that made me believe every story she told. She knew how to draw me out too.

I hadn't tried my story on anyone new for a while, and I was surprised at how it was received—with approval, with affirmation, with congratulations even, for having given myself permission to step away from the past. Several Santa Feans predicted we'd soon be neighbors, that I'd be pulling up my roots "back East" and moving to New Mexico. I didn't see that in my future, but I loved being in a place where people didn't find my story to be at all unlike other stories they knew. I began to wonder if it was an East Coast practice to put people into boxes according to the kind of work they do. Or maybe I was the one who felt the need for a label, a title, a legitimate explanation for who I was in the world.

And then there were the stories that came with the art. Well-documented stories at the Georgia O'Keeffe Museum about her time in Taos and Abiquiú. Mexican *dichos*, or proverbs, in two separate exhibitions. In the New Mexico Museum of Art, folk wisdom was scrawled beneath primitive-style paintings, offering the kind of fortune cookie advice we all grew up with, regardless of language or culture. In the Museum of International Folk Art, a maze of rooms was filled with photographs of words and symbols tattooed on cars, trucks, and buses throughout Latin America, their messages ranging from romantic to lewd, from devout to sacrilegious (or both at once, depending on how you interpret eighteen-wheelers with mud flaps bearing images of the Virgin Mary).

On Canyon Road, gallery owners and artists talked about the light, the energy of the artistic community, and why they would never work anywhere else again. I filled the better part of three days meandering up and down that steep lane, studying paintings and sculptures and taking inspiration from the artist bios.

I discovered stories about saints imported to New Mexico by Spanish conquistadors and Franciscan friars, and about saint makers, or *santeros*, who'd brought those saints to life in the New World, using wood and paint. Stories about the inexplicably beautiful spiral staircase in Loretto Chapel, which reaches from floor to choir loft in what appears to be one magnificent piece, as if the mysterious carpenter who built it and then vanished had peeled a giant wooden apple in one long curl and suspended its unbroken skin between heaven and earth. Stories about people who lived here before the conquistadors and the friars came—and who live here still—including my favorite, a story about the Native American tradition of holding a "baby's first laugh party" to mark an infant's passage into the world of shared laughter.

Even the food came with stories, the cultural and culinary overtones as richly layered as the Santa Fe shepherd's pie, featuring jalapenos and squash, I enjoyed on my last evening. Although my casita had a kitchenette, I had abandoned all thoughts of using it after that first stroll through town on an empty stomach. Why cook when there were so many tempting places to dine? Why stay in when people everywhere were happy to strike up conversations?

Since I'd stopped working, I'd been eating more meals than ever by myself. I'd done plenty of solo traveling in the past and had no qualms about requesting a table for one. But in my experience, a single diner often made the wait staff and other diners squirm. Not in Santa Fe.

In the hotel's breakfast room, a family drew me into their morning conversations about local galleries and museums. In Burro Alley, I discovered Paris Café, tucked behind a life-sized bronze burro and boasting an authentic French menu. I chatted with a woman at the outdoor table beside mine, another solo diner, who ordered champagne for one without the least self-consciousness. I put that on a to-do list for another trip.

Dragon Phoenix Pearls—suggestive of a story of international jewelry thieves—was the name of the jasmine tea I sipped at the Teahouse at the top of Canyon Road. A twelve-page menu provided biographic details on each available tealeaf—black or green, red or brown. Cup in hand, I perched on an overstuffed, undersprung sofa and surveyed the maze of small rooms. I was surrounded by people who were busy scribbling in journals or tapping away on laptops. Only then did I begin to fantasize about moving to Santa Fe, spending days at the Teahouse with my stories spread around me, a supply of sharp pencils at one elbow, a steaming pot of tea at the other. I would let my hair grow long and go silver (not gray), drape myself in one of those elegant wraps Santa Fe women wear so well, maybe even acquire a pair of stylish boots. I let myself try on that story, at least until my little teapot ran dry.

In the Mexican restaurant Los Mayas, I had an out-of-country experience. Two sixtyish Mexican gentlemen took their places on a small riser and began to strum guitars to the delight of the alfresco dinner crowd. After a few flamenco-style numbers, they slyly slipped into a tongue-in-cheek medley of "Give My Regards to Broadway," "In the Good Old Summertime," and "Take Me Out to the Ballgame." Cute, I thought—they're playing up to the American tourists. Wait a minute, I thought—that's me. Oh, and by the way, I'm still in America—a fact I had temporarily forgotten, transported as I was by the music, the food, and perhaps the sangria. I recalled my walking tour of the city, how our guide had noted that New Mexico is the only state with a license plate that includes "USA" because so many visitors still confuse it with "old Mexico."

On my last day, I had just one task on my list: a farewell tour of Canyon Road, with the intention of buying a single piece of art. What image would I choose? I flirted with a landscape by a transplanted New Yorker—to me his paintings of New Mexico evoked the mountains of western Ireland; he said I wasn't the first to make that unlikely connection. I wandered off to another gallery, then another and another for the rest of the afternoon, making a short list of paintings I might like to have.

In the end, I bought an unframed image titled "Out of the Shadows," an encaustic on wood, small enough to tuck into my carry-on bag. It's a perfect little painting that tells a perfectly incomplete story: the silhouette of a girl in a doorway, shoulders squared and hands held straight at her sides, as if she is about to step forward. Only her slightly turned-in right foot suggests she has paused at a threshold. Behind her is a tree trunk, flashes of green that suggest a garden, a brick wall dappled with sunlight. The foreground and doorway are less clear, yet still inviting; the fused colors suggest a fluid path ahead. I don't know why the girl hesitates; perhaps she is uncertain of what will happen next, or perhaps she is simply savoring that liminal space. But I knew in an instant she would be going home with me.

I also came home from Santa Fe with a soundtrack for remembering my visit. One afternoon I followed the sounds of a flute into a small shop full of musical instruments, and there I discovered Red Skyhawk, this time in jeans. I thanked him for his music on the first night of the story festival. I noticed some of his recordings were for sale. He played a few tracks from a CD called "Blessings," recorded with his friend Ken Pintewa Estrada. He inscribed the liner of the copy I bought with the words "Ota Yawaste," which translates as "Many Blessings." As good a phrase as any to sum up my first trip to Santa Fe.

I came home from Santa Fe with a suitcase full of stories—the same ones I left with, the many I heard there, and this one too. A story of renewal. A story about what happens when you let your story go out to play in a city where it can't help bumping into, and being enriched by, other people's stories. A story about what happens when you begin to tell your story over and over—to people you've never met—in a way that lets you hear it for yourself in a new way, lets you detect the confidence in your own voice as you talk about why you left that old job, why you've lingered so long at a threshold, and what you've learned about yourself during all the time you've been standing there.

I came home from Santa Fe with the knowledge that going to Santa Fe is not the kind of thing you can cross off your list once you've done it. Or you could, but then you'd just have to start a new list and write "Go back to Santa Fe" right at the top.

I did go back—as soon as I'd worked at my new job in a nonprofit arts agency long enough to earn a little vacation time. I went back with a few of my stories having already found their way out into the world and a few new ones tucked between the layers of clothes in my suitcase, confident that a change of scenery would do them a world of good.

That Breathless Charm

They've practiced their socks off learning meringue, rumba, tango, swing, and foxtrot. Fifth-grade boys and girls who wouldn't have touched each other in March now comfortably coax each other around the stage.

His periwinkle shoes have a texture that suggests the skin of a reptile. His feet are long, and it's a lot of periwinkle to take in all at once, even with the considerable distraction of the powder-blue suit that hangs from his lanky frame. Loose is how he looks—confident, and ready to begin.

Introductions have been made, the dancers are positioned more or less evenly on the stage, and Miss Victoria is just now quieting the standing-room-only crowd. The music begins and she waits a few beats. "Five, six, seven, eight," she breathes into the microphone, and twenty-eight feet burst into a foxtrot. The auditorium erupts with cheers, applause, and shrieks. Cameras flash from every corner.

Up on the stage, I have the advantage of seeing every dancer at close range, watching footwork fancy and not-so, and feeling the full range of emotions—joy through angst—written on the faces of fourteen underage foxtrotters. I want to know who to thank for the brilliant musical selection, Frank Sinatra's rendition of "The Way You Look Tonight," which is literally and metaphorically soaring over the heads of the ten- and eleven-year-old dancers, as I swipe at tears and try to give all seven couples my full attention.

Some girls are a foot taller than their partners, requiring the boys to tilt their heads at awkward angles to maintain eye contact and avoid staring into the budding breasts of classmates. While some dancers blush, others can't stop grinning. While some glide, others shuffle. Some audibly count steps, while others hum along to the music. The boy in blue is one smooth dancer; the periwinkle shoes saunter through the slow steps and sprint through the fast ones.

Chicken wings up, toes facing toes, look like you're having fun. For ten weeks, twenty sessions in all, they've heard this mantra again and again. They've practiced their socks off learning meringue, rumba, tango, swing, and foxtrot. Fifth-grade boys and girls who wouldn't have touched each other in March now comfortably coax each other around the stage, most in nearly perfect time with the music, hands firmly gripping shoulder blades or lightly touching bra straps.

It's a warm May afternoon at the J. W. Catherine School on the southwestern edge of Philadelphia. Many students in this school—like their counterparts from the six other schools represented here today—live at or below the poverty level. Still, their parents have managed to dress them neatly, modestly, proudly for this special occasion—the 2009 Dancing Classrooms Philly Semifinal Competition.

Ballroom dance instructors have taught the children to behave like ladies and gentlemen, at least on stage; back in their seats, they're far more exuberant as they cheer on classmates in the other dances. Each team has a color, worn in wide sashes by the young ladies, spelled out on laminated sheets safety-pinned to the backs of jackets and shirts for the young men.

I wonder where that boy found a dress shirt in exactly the shade (Flyers' orange) of his partner's sash. I'm drawn to a skinny girl who looks like her grandmother just fixed her up for church on Easter: a simple dress with a hint of lace at the knees, tights and shiny shoes, all topped off with a thick knit cape that can't quite camouflage her bony shoulders. Every stitch of her clothing is snow white, interrupted only by a red sash. She's not the best dancer on the stage, but she's clearly having fun.

The students have been coached to put a lot of hip motion into the Latin dances, and they've taken this instruction to heart. Parents all but swoon over the tango and gasp as their daughters mime sexy moves by pulling splayed fingers back across their foreheads. The rumba (or "roooooomba," as Miss Victoria says) teams really sell it. Hips in every size and shape sway, wiggle, or jerk, displaying a vast array of abilities.

The auditorium was warm even before the dancing began, and now someone has flung open the doors at the back and side of the hall. Neighbors poke their heads in to see what all the commotion is, then stay to watch as the swing teams kick up their heels to "Hit the Road Jack" while the audience belts out the lyrics. One dimpled, dark-haired boy in a crisp tan shirt stands just a few inches taller than my four-year-old nephew. He's giving it all he's got—and he's got plenty—and when the music stops I'm tempted to pick him up and hug him.

But then I remember I'm one of the judges, and aside from the need to comport myself as an impartial observer, I've only got a few seconds to finalize my scores for this round.

It's so hard to assign numbers to what's going on here. Each couple gets a score from 6 to 10. The 6s and 10s reveal themselves within the first several seconds of each dance, but my pencil hovers nervously over every 7, 8, and 9 before I commit to a score. Seven couples per dance, seven numbers to circle before the music stops, two sets of each dance, three busy judges. We dodge dancers, circle numbers, turn in score sheets. Then a new group takes the stage, and we do it all over again. There's no time to compare notes or remember the scores we've given from one round to the next. Like everyone else in the auditorium, we'll learn which two teams will advance to the finals at the end of the program when all 210 team scores have been tallied.

My dance-related qualifications for being here are marginal: my Dad and I were finalists in the jitterbug contest at a high school father-daughter dance in 1976; come to think of it, my three sisters all were finalists in the same event with the same partner in subsequent years, so Dad probably deserves the credit there. Also, I'm related to the McNiff Twins of Irish step-dancing fame; OK, they're not really famous and "McNiff" is just how our last name was mispronounced at an event one long-ago St. Patrick's Day. I did, however, watch my youngest sisters and their peers perform countless times during their grade school years, so I appreciate the hard work involved in making these dances look easy. I recognize the joy streaming toward the stage from parents and teachers. (And I did learn, some decades afterwards, that there really was a famous group of Irish step dancers named McNiff.)

I'm lucky enough to be here as a judge because of my newish

job at a nonprofit arts agency in Philadelphia. Dancing Classrooms Philly—modeled on the New York City program featured in the 2005 documentary *Mad Hot Ballroom*—is one of a hundred or so arts organizations I've had the privilege to work with in that role. I truly believe in the magic this program offers to Philadelphia schoolchildren, and it turns out that matters more than dancing skills when it comes to being a judge.

Anyway, even an untrained eye can assess the criteria we've been given. I still want to give every couple a ten. It helps only slightly to know that each student will go home with a ribbon and the afternoon will end with one big rainbow of a line dance that includes them all.

The second round of foxtrotting ended fifteen minutes ago, but I've got Old Blue Eyes and Young Blue Shoes under my skin, and I'm still feeling the glow. To the great delight of the home team supporters, the Catherine School has advanced to the finals, along with the Spring Garden School.

Part of me wishes these young people could stay in this moment forever. But they will, of course, change, and so will I. But I'll never, ever hear that song again without recalling the eager faces, those periwinkle shoes, and the way that little girl's face lit up when I told her I liked her cape on my way out the door.

Shopping Spree • mixed media collage on watercolor paper

Consignments

> *con·sign (k?n-s?n') v. –signed, -signing, -signs – tr. 1. To give over to the care of another; entrust. 2. To turn over permanently to another's charge or to a lasting condition; commit irrevocably. 3. To deliver (merchandise, for example) for custody or sale. 4. To set apart, as for special use or purpose; assign.*
>
> —The American Heritage Dictionary of the English Language, fourth edition

4.

ONE FINE DAY LAST SPRING, I ASSIGNED MYSELF THE TASK of making my peace, once and for all, with the little red dress. I set apart time to spend with the dress, to see it for what it is: a mere few yards of polyester, lined with a few more yards of polyester; purchased for a not-too-considerable sum after more-than-considerable window shopping and dressing-room angst; worn once, ten summers ago, for one unenchanted evening at the end of what had seemed a promising week; then consigned to a closet, an attic, and finally—or so I thought—a second-hand shop.

For most of its life, the little red dress has been consigned to languish in the attic of my little white house. It's been there almost since arriving in the United States from its country of origin, Indonesia, then traveling with me briefly across the US border, deep into the Canadian Rockies, and home again to Pennsylvania.

On that rare day of liberation last spring, I removed the dress from its plastic garment bag. I suspended it from my office door so I could inspect it at close range, describe its simple but classic lines to you, convince you there is nothing wrong with it, no reason why someone shouldn't have purchased it, new or gently (ever-so-gently) used.

No doubt I expected too much of the little red dress from the beginning. Not the dress, perhaps, but the occasion for which it was purchased. Or not the occasion exactly, but the man associated with it. I mistakenly set this dear little dress aside for special use, imbued it with qualities he—I mean it—simply did not possess, and inadvertently set off a chain of events I later came to regret. In the end, the occasion turned out to be oh-so-ordinary and the man a complete and utter disappointment, despite all the care I had taken in making my selection.

This is not about that man. Or it is about him, but only to the extent that our fleeting dalliance made me doubt, for some time after, my own judgment, my taste, my discernment—and not just in clothing. I did try him on, I admit it. I even took him home, briefly. But I never took the tags off, although I might have if he'd hung around. Never mind that I later realized what a colossal mistake that would have been. And a man is the not the kind of thing you can drop off at the local consignment shop once buyer's remorse sets in.

So being left with only the little red dress was not the worst possible outcome of that sorry episode in my history, a history in which the man himself has now been set apart, consigned to the status of a mere footnote. I do apologize if I've aroused your curiosity, but I have nothing else to say about the man. Not one moment of the time we spent together is worth recounting. All the best bits took place in my imagination, I'm sorry to say. I trust you've had a similar experience somewhere along the way.

Still, for an entire decade I was unable to separate the objective appeal of that little red dress from the unhappy associations formed on the one and only time I wore it. Which is not to say I spent ten years carrying those thoughts around with me, day after day, month after month. The little red dress only ever crossed my mind if I went to the attic looking for something else. On those rare occasions, the old associations would flit through my mind, along with mild pangs of regret—not about my failed relationship with the man, but about my failed relationship with the little red dress.

I did wear that dress well, if I do say so myself. I've never been a little-black-dress kind of a girl; I've always been partial to colors, and the deep cherry hue looked fine against my pale skin and my reddish-brown hair. Its tailored lines hugged me gently, without being too clingy. I liked how I looked when I tried it on, and I liked how I felt when I wore it that one time. Still, I decided long ago I had no further use for the dress. Yet I cannot seem to wash my hands of it, try as I might. Lady Macbeth springs to mind, no doubt because of the blood-red hue of the synthetically soft fabric.

I assure you, though, this is more comedy than tragedy. There are no stains, of any type, on my little red dress.

3.

For years I'd walked and driven past the consignment shop without so much as a second-hand thought. When clothes no longer fit my body or my taste but were still fit to be worn, I donated them to one of the charities that called periodically and offered to take them off my hands. Or I dropped them off at a hospital thrift shop, feeling satisfied that my unused but usable clothing might generate a few dollars for a worthy cause.

My first pass at consigning clothes was mostly a symbolic gesture. I had recently made my escape from the business world and had the luxury of time between jobs to rethink my relationship to work—and indirectly, my relationship to clothes, since I no longer had to put myself into the world on a daily basis looking "professional." I was, in fact, so-very-in-between-jobs that I had no idea what I would do next for employment. But I knew it wouldn't be more of the same, and I felt confident I could let go of the trappings of that old life, beginning with suits and blouses, skirts and dresses, especially those that had a corporate whiff about them. And while I hadn't reached a stage of being unemployed where I was overly concerned about my finances, I liked the idea of picking up a little extra cash by recycling my old business attire.

So one day while I was out running errands, I dropped by the local consignment shop to observe what was on the racks and to inquire about the process for selling clothes there. I browsed through the merchandise and left with a printed page of rules tucked into my purse. Within a few weeks I returned with an inaugural basketful of clothes to offer to the shopkeepers.

The little red dress—already five years old—was not among the items I brought with me that first time. I don't know why. Perhaps at that point I had perceived only the possibility of redeeming my unwanted apparel for pin money. It had not yet occurred to me that other types of redemption might be available through the consignment shop.

I stood and watched as the twenty-something girl behind the counter sifted through my basket, spending no more than two or three seconds on each item before consigning it to one of two piles. I'd studied the guidelines and brought only items I felt had a chance to be taken, although I confess several were well beyond the no-more-than-two-years-old rule. To my great satisfaction, some of those older pieces landed in the "yes" pile. The girl had encouraged me to wander around the shop while she went through my things, but I had demurred, opting instead to watch as she made her snap decisions. I felt a little thrill each time she placed an item into the good pile, and an oddly personal sense of rejection each time she discarded an item, even though I had already rejected each of those items myself, for one reason or another.

Some time later, after I'd become an experienced consigner, I dropped into the shop on a quiet Sunday afternoon and asked the manager, Sarah, to educate me about her business. I learned that many customers do take rejections personally and try to debate the merits of their offered items. But to no avail; overall guidelines are handed down by a corporate office that manages six consignment shops, and each member of the staff not only knows the guidelines, but is intimately familiar with what's already on the floor, what's in back waiting to be processed, what's currently selling and what is not. Quick decisions are essential because on any given day thousands of items may be delivered for consideration, and hundreds likely will be accepted. There is only so much space in the back room, there are only so many weeks in each season, and there are only so many customers interested in used turtlenecks or high-end designer shoes. Still, about 80 percent of accepted items do sell, so the snap decision makers apparently know their stuff.

A few days after my first items were accepted, a contract was slipped through my mail slot, indicating the terms of consignment: sixty days in the shop, at the end of which I could either reclaim any unsold items or abandon them for good; a 40 percent commission on items sold, to be paid by check a few weeks after the claim date; and no responsibility on the part of management for any items that inadvertently went missing on their watch.

On day fifty-nine, I returned to the shop, contract in hand, and learned to my delight that several items had sold. The counter girl *du jour* highlighted a printout for me so I could see what had not sold and could collect those items myself from the racks, using the coding system on the labels.

Net proceeds of my first foray into consigning: about $40, minus $5 or so for gas and parking meters. Not much, but I wasn't really in it for the money. I'd discovered I liked the game. Emboldened by my modest beginner's success, I determined to fill another basket in time for the autumn wave of consignments.

2.

One of the many things my little red dress has going for it is that it is a dress for all seasons, despite being a sleeveless sheath. The rich red color makes it perfect for the winter holidays, yet it's lightweight enough for, say, a dinner in early August in a far northern clime, perhaps with a chic wrap thrown around one's shoulders to protect against a sudden downward shift in temperature (or mood).

And oh, how that dress travels. I had tucked it into my suitcase between layers of tissue paper and managed to keep it sequestered for days from hiking boots and ever-increasing piles of dirty clothes. Only one night on the trip called for cocktail attire, and when at last I extracted my little red dress from its tissue, it looked as good as it had in the dressing room; not so much as the whisper of a wrinkle betrayed the rough company it had been keeping. The hemline just caressed the tops of my knees. The wrap was a perfect complement, its muted print in red and gold and gray. Flat black shoes dialed down the look just a notch to match the setting—the upscale dining room of a well-appointed mountain resort.

The next time I delivered clothes to the consignment shop I filled two laundry baskets, requiring separate trips to the parking lot. As I returned with the second load—which contained the little red dress, casually mixed in with its attic-mates, *sans* tissue paper—the girl behind the counter asked: "Have you consigned with us before?" I replied that I had, once, and she offered a compliment: "You really seem to have a good feel for what we're looking for." The reject pile from the first load was quite small.

I watched as the salesgirl dipped into my second basket of

clothes, her hands and eyes simultaneously making their quick assessments, deciding what was likely to sell, weighing each item against the inventory already crammed into overflowing racks; accepting, rejecting, accepting. I waited eagerly for her to discover my little red dress. My breath caught for a split second as she plucked it from the basket. Was it my imagination or did her fingers linger admiringly on the well-made darts for just a moment longer than it took her to decide?

In an instant the deed was done. The little red dress—and the miscalculations and missteps it had come to represent—was placed on top of the "yes" pile. My selection, my judgment, my taste regarding this particular garment had been validated. The dress had been consigned, irrevocably committed, permanently removed from my possession. As I left the shop with my receipt and my nearly empty laundry baskets, I stifled the urge to pump a fist in the air. The little red dress, my little red albatross, was no longer my concern. A burden had been lifted from my shoulders.

1.

Day 58. I couldn't stand the suspense. I had to know that someone else had taken possession of my little red dress. I had entrusted it to a bevy of part-time caretakers who stood behind that counter for more than eight weeks; who steam-cleaned, catalogued, and rotated merchandise to keep it moving; who made room in the 2,000-square-foot store for a never-ending influx of used clothing, second thoughts, overly optimistic sizes, and poorly chosen gifts; who surfed daily the tidal wave of fleeting styles, passing fancies, imagined scenes that never transpired, choices made, poses struck, once-in-a-lifetime outfits, and too many garments to count still sheepishly trailing telltale original sales tags from their sleeves or waistbands.

As the printer spat out the updated list of my consignments, I glanced toward the elevated rack on the far wall, the one with dresses, suits, and gowns, hoping not to see a flash of red. I didn't. But as the girl highlighted the page for me, even upside down I could see she'd made a thick yellow streak right through the hieroglyphic that read **WDR 12 RED JCHAUS POLY SL LG $18.00**, indicating my little red dress (women's size 12, from Josephine Chaus) had not been sold. How was that possible? It was (is) the perfect little red dress, in perfect condition, perfectly suited to someone else's wardrobe (life), the readiest ready-to-wear little red dress you ever could imagine.

And yet there it was, mixed in with the other dress-up clothes—unpurchased, unchosen, rejected by two whole months' worth of customers—and once again on its way to being consigned to my drafty attic. Oh why hadn't someone else bought my little red dress before I'd had to reclaim it?

I began to wonder if the dress gave off bad vibes. I began to wonder if there could be such a thing as a cautionary dress, destined to remain in my possession for the rest of my days, urging me to think twice before making another bold move in the direction of romance, a move like the one that had left me holding only a garment bag full of crimson polyester.

As I reached for the hanger, I thought I detected the faint outline of a smirk where once I had seen only a jewel neckline. With a sinking feeling, I gathered the red dress and my few other unsold items into my arms, presented them at the counter to be cross-checked against the list, and headed back to the car, despondent. I'd cleared nearly $80 on my second round of consignments. But I still hadn't unloaded the little red dress.

After just a few months as a consigner, I'd developed a system. Whatever sold, sold, and whatever didn't was donated to the next charity that asked for used clothing. With one exception, of course. I couldn't bring myself to simply give away the little red dress, and not only because it wasn't the kind of thing you offered to someone in need. I wanted, no needed, for someone else to choose it, to take it home.

Sarah told me most of her consigners do not reclaim their unsold items, but instead allow the shop to give them directly to charities or sell them in flea markets, the proceeds of which are then donated to good causes. Consignment shops are, I have learned, very "green"; they throw away almost nothing and see themselves as straddling two industries—recycling and retailing. They do toss small personal effects they sometimes find in pockets or purses, like business cards, pills, and pens.

Back in my attic, I slipped the garment bag over the little red dress. I tucked it between other clothes I no longer wear but don't want to part with or can't give away because they are so terribly out of date. For months at a time I forgot the little red dress was even there.

I kept consigning, even after I found a new job and had to carve time out of my weekends to shuttle clothes back and forth to the shop. Consigning has taught me to resist impulse clothing purchases, to consider how many times I might have to schlep an item up and down the stairs as seasons change or over to the consignment shop if I change my mind. Still, my backlog of extraneous clothes is seemingly undepletable, and once or twice a year I still scrape together the minimum number of consignable items (ten), with generally good results, except when I reach too far back into the past and forget about the no-shoulder-pads rule.

Two more times in the intervening years I have slipped that little red dress into a bundle of clothes, confident it would be rescued from the rack on its second trip through the shop, or surely its third. Each time whichever girl was behind the counter looked at the dress approvingly, leading me to feel certain I would not only be validated, but vindicated, at last.

I had, you must understand, nothing to lose by trying again and so much more to gain than the $7.20 the dress would fetch for me if it sold.

Three times now my little red dress has been readily accepted for consignment. Three times I have found it waiting for me, emitting the merest hint of smugness—or is it resignation?—as I lift it from the rack, reclaiming it, rechoosing it, unable to abandon it.

I asked Sarah if she had any way to know if a customer—a hypothetical customer, that is—brought the same item in more than once. She surprised me by saying that sometimes she actually encourages a customer to try again, especially with high-end or classic items. When I confessed to having brought the same *classic* little red dress into her shop on three separate occasions, she smiled and admitted that if an item doesn't sell the first time, it probably never will. But she doesn't mind if someone keeps trying. The only thing that annoys her is when someone brings in items that are blatantly damaged.

It's been months now since I moved the dress from my attic down to the second floor, for what I thought was an afternoon visit. Mostly I've left it hanging—free of its white plastic bag—in a closet with the few dresses and suits I still wear in a life that is decidedly more casual than it used to be. More than once I've taken the dress out and draped it over the door again, essaying to discern what I might from those few yards of fabric. Only once during those months have I offered a new round of clothes for consignment and the little red dress was not among them.

One crisp fall day, on a whim, I decided to try on the little red dress again, just to see what might happen. I slipped out of shapeless black sweat pants and a green corduroy shirt. I unzipped the little red dress and let it slide over my neck and settle on my shoulders. The cool lining slinked along my torso until it reached my hips, where a bit more coaxing was required than what I remembered from ten years earlier. I stepped out into the hallway and faced the mirror. Not bad, I thought, even if it is a little snug. Not bad at all.

I only kept it on for a minute or two, but in that brief time I began to understand what my little red dress had been trying to tell me ever since that first trip to the consignment shop: We belong together, we have a future, it's not too late. Other occasions are just waiting for us to show up, arm in sleevehole. I blushed with shame to think how I'd let a mere man come between me and my little red dress, quite nearly for keeps.

As I reached behind me to undo the zipper, the plastic tab from the consignment shop label scratched a soft spot just below my left armpit. I ought to take that tag off, I suppose. So my little red dress will be ready the next time I need it. It is not going back to the consignment shop. In fact it's not going anywhere ever again without me inside it—ideally, me minus about six or seven pounds.

What was I thinking, trying to consign my little red dress to someone else's life? As if she—I mean it—could go out into the world for me in search of acceptance, redemption, adventure, maybe even love.

I am no longer sure if the little red dress has been entrusted to me, or if I've been entrusted to it. But we seem to be stuck with each other, consigned to each other's care.

Half Remembered • acrylic and collage on museum board

Somebody Almost

My twenty-year-old self recognized something in the words of this particular poem, a lesson I hadn't yet had to apply to my own life, at least not in any profound way. But on some level, I understood that lesson and filed it away.

TWO YEARS BEFORE SHE DIED AT THE AGE OF SEVENTY, I had the privilege of seeing Ntozake Shange up close for the first time, listening as she read old and new poems to an auditorium packed with (mostly female) admirers at the African American Museum in Philadelphia. The occasion was the opening of an exhibition at the museum celebrating the fortieth anniversary of Shange's 1976 groundbreaking "choreopoem": "For Colored Girls Who Have Considered Suicide/When the Rainbow Is Enuf." Ms. Shange looked so frail it was hard to believe she was only ten years older than me; I learned later that she'd had a series of strokes about a decade earlier. But her voice was still strong, and her words, although I hadn't actively sought them out in many years, still had the power to yank me back to an earlier time—in my life, in the world, in my evolution as a reader, a writer, a woman.

Ms. Shange had no way of knowing that the middle-aged white woman on the aisle seat of the fourth row had a cherished, yellowed paperback edition of "For Colored Girls" in her purse, heavily annotated in blue ink with asterisks and checkmarks, underscores and brackets. Or that nearly four decades earlier, when she was an occasional contributor to her college newspaper, *The Villanovan*, an editor had handed her two press tickets to see the still-new play performed in the small studio space of Philadelphia's Walnut

Street Theatre and asked her to write a review. This assignment had both flattered and terrified me. I loved theater, and even as an underclassman, I'd likely read (and maybe even seen) as many plays as anyone else on the paper's staff. It was a short train ride into the city, and I knew I could talk a friend into joining me for this cultural adventure. But writing a review? Criticizing someone's art? Who was I to judge another's writing? And then to hand in that judgment and see it sent out into the world (OK, not the great wide, world, just Villanova's campus) in black and white? Who was I?

I was an English major, for one thing, and while I was open to the experience of seeing an experimental theater piece, even before I got on that train, I was a bit distracted by Shange's unconventional spellings, beginning with the odd-looking "enuf" in her title. "For Colored Girls" is unabashedly Black and feminist, at times searing in its language and shocking in the realities it portrays. As the play began, it occurred to me that I was, perhaps, both too green (as a woman, as a feminist, as a writer) and too white (as a second-generation, Irish-Catholic, middle class, commuter from a suburban college sometimes referred to back in the 1970s as "Vanillanova") to even begin to understand what was happening on that stage, never mind being there in the guise of a theater critic.

And yet, in the way that art often does, almost from the moment those seven rainbow-clad ladies took their places and began to speak, they drew me into their dance, into their stories. Their language, their movements, their confidence, their vulnerabilities, their secrets, their sassiness—so unlike mine in oh-so-many ways, but surprisingly familiar in others. Who in that audience—or in any audience, anywhere—had not at some point experienced unrequited love? I couldn't help but see myself in the spotlight when the Lady in Red stepped forward and announced:

> "without any assistance or guidance from you
> i have loved you assiduously for 8 months 2wks &
> a day
> i have been stood up four times
> i've left 7 packages on yr doorstep
> forty poems 2 plants & 3 handmade notecards i left
> town so i cd send..."

But it was the Lady in Green who spoke to me most clearly that night. And it is the Lady in Green who has continued to speak to me—sometimes in a whisper, sometimes in a roar—down through the years. When she stepped forward and began her raw, funny, angry, self-affirming poem toward the end of the play, her words turned the key in a lock somewhere deep inside me.

> "somebody almost walked off wid alla my stuff
> not my poems or a dance I gave up in the street
> but somebody almost walked off wid alla my stuff..."

My twenty-year-old self recognized something in the words of this particular poem, a lesson I hadn't yet had to apply to my own life, at least not in any profound way. But on some level, I understood that lesson and filed it away. Only over time would I begin to collect experiences where my sense of self—and self-worth—as a woman would truly be tested. Sometimes, as in the poem, by a man, in a personal relationship. Other times by a job, especially in the years I spent as a ghost writer when I often felt like the Lady in Green: "my stuff is the anonymous ripped off/treasure of the year." Occasionally by a bully in the workplace (and not always a man) or a contractor looking to take advantage of me as a homeowner.

Over time, just the two words "somebody almost" began to buzz in my ear when I sensed that someone was perhaps trying to take more from me than I was willing to give, or taking credit for something I had done, or gently (or not so gently) trying to mold me into some version of a self who didn't feel authentic. This little alarm didn't always sound in time to save me from being hurt or from making a bad decision. But it has never failed me in those moments when I've most needed to remember who I am or who I am still trying to become. And for that, I have always felt a debt of gratitude to Ms. Shange, and to her Lady in Green.

I didn't read the text of "For Colored Girls" until some time after I'd seen that performance and written my review. I know this because my paperback edition is dated 1980, which was a year or two after my brief turn as a theater critic. I no longer recall what I wrote in that review; I am sure it was positive, although I doubt it was terribly insightful. My old clips from *The Villanovan* were wrecked years ago when a pipe broke and the storage locker in my apartment complex was flooded. I do know that when I wrote that review I couldn't possibly pretend (and still can't) to understand the world through the eyes of a woman of color. But I also know that seeing that play at that time in my life informed my understanding of myself and other women I knew then or have met since. It made me think differently about our choices, our challenges, our strengths, our triumphs.

That old paperback copy of *For Colored Girls* has traveled with me through the decades. Occasionally, I've pulled it from a bookshelf, flipped through it, and retraced my own trail of marked-up lines from beginning to end. I'm knocked off balance every time I reread these lines from the Lady in Green:

> ...i gotta have me in my pocket/to get
> round like a good woman shd/& make the poem in
> the pot or the chicken in the dance/what I got to do
> I gotta have my stuff to do it...

Tucked into the pages of my well-worn book is an April 1982 interview from the *Wilmington News Journal* with Shange, who had recently done a reading at the University of Delaware, just miles from my first apartment. The headline describes her as "An artist in search of personal liberation, not fame." The article discusses her upper-middle-class origins in Trenton, where she was known as Paulette Williams before she renamed herself; it also discusses her feminism, which was not at all hindered by a general fondness for men; her struggles against racism and sexism; and the challenge of wanting her words simply to speak for themselves at a time when the success of *For Colored Girls* had the entertainment industry clamoring for more. That article also explains that the name Ms. Shange chose for herself comes from Zulu. Much later I learned the meaning behind her adopted name: Ntozake means "she who has her own things" and Shange means "she who walks with lions."

I reread *For Colored Girls* in its entirety before I saw Ntozake Shange in Philadelphia back in 2016, and again when I heard she had died—a loss that hit me harder than I might have expected. The news of her passing sent me searching for more information about her life and her writing in all those years between 2018 and that long-ago day when a college newspaper editor handed me two tickets to a play I'd never heard of. What I found through that search was one of those little gifts the universe sometimes offers up: In Ntozake Shange's official biography, listed among her academic credits, right there between Rice and DePaul, is Villanova University, where for a time she taught writing. It seemed funny I hadn't known this sooner because I retain a keen interest in the goings-on at my alma mater. But discovering when I did that Villanova had a place in Ms. Shange's story, too, felt like a kind of blessing. It felt like a nod from the frail but esteemed poet on that stage in 2016 to the woman seated in the fourth row, intentionally dressed in green.

Revision, Like Launching a Marble Boat

I've kept one of Tiger's gifts for nearly thirty-five years because in itself it is a treasure, but also because it holds a riddle it took me forever to solve.

LATELY I FIND MYSELF LESS INTIMIDATED BY THE BLANK page (screen) and more by the thought of revising something I've already written. Not something in the early stages—usually when I've got a new project underway, I can't wait to get back to it. The revisions I dread, or at least postpone far longer than I should, are on work I've already sent out into the world, one way or another. Writing I've workshoped at a conference, with feedback that now must be weighed. Writing I've submitted to literary journals that has been rejected often enough—even if some rejections have been encouraging—that I know I must reopen the file, reread my own work, and wrestle with my pages.

Of course the ease with which we make revisions these days—and here I am talking about the mechanical ease of editing a document through the magic of word-processing software, not the mental work that goes into rewriting—is something most of us take for granted. But it hasn't always been that way. I used a manual typewriter—and gallons of whiteout—in high school. I pecked my way through college papers on an electric typewriter, which fortunately had a ribbon of corrective tape because I've always been a lousy typist.

My first job after college was as a medical writer in a teaching hospital where I worked with staff physicians and visiting fellows and residents to polish their research papers, book chapters, and presentations. We were lucky enough to have in our office one of the three word-processing machines in the hospital; it was about the size of a Mini Cooper, and only two people in our four-person department were even allowed to touch it. I wasn't one of them. My job was to write on or mark up paper, sometimes to literally cut and paste (with scissors and tape), then turn the pages over to one of the girls whose job it was to type or revise documents. In the 1980s, this was cutting-edge technology. Our machine was a Vydec, and he (we four women all agreed the big lug was a "he") was both a technological wonder and a highly temperamental coworker. At least once a week, Vydec acted up and we had to call in a technician. Still, we cranked out a lot of medical papers on that old machine, and the doctors were not at all shy about asking for one more set of revisions before we sent their pages out into the world. They took to word processing like ducks to water.

With one exception—Tiger John, a surgeon from China who spent about three years with us as an international fellow. He was one of the first physicians permitted to leave China after the Cultural Revolution, and he was in the US to learn about Western medicine so he could bring new knowledge back home. He couldn't practice here, but he could watch surgeries, observe clinics, and attend conferences. And since everyone around him was writing papers, he thought he'd try that too.

Everyone loved Tiger, who was nothing like his name. He was gentle and extraordinarily polite. And he was constantly offering us small gifts from China. I've kept one of Tiger's gifts for nearly thirty-five years because in itself it is a treasure, but also because it holds a riddle it took me forever to solve. It's a small rectangle of silk, printed with the image of a large marble boat. Tiger explained it was a real boat, made of marble, from a long time ago. But with his limited English (and my nonexistent Mandarin), he couldn't make me understand how a marble boat could float. It was a marvel, for sure. But our conversation about it ended—as many of our conversations did—with me nodding my head, him bowing, and both of us grinning, pretending we'd managed to communicate more than we actually had.

Lately, I've been feeling like making myself sit down to start a revision is like trying to make a marble boat float—impossible. The longer I wait, the more I convince myself I'll be disappointed with my writing and—because I mostly write personal essays—with my life.

Revision always reminds me of Tiger John, although not in the best way. Tiger took to word processing like a marble boat takes to water. He used a manual typewriter, and when he was satisfied with a draft, he would bring a fresh pile of pages to me as if it were another of his gifts. His typing was worse than mine, and with little English at his command, his manuscripts were incomprehensible. I'd read through his pages, making edits and scribbling questions in the margins, drawing arrows to indicate which paragraphs might be moved where. We'd discuss—as best we could—what I had understood and what he had intended. Then I'd mark up the pages some more and turn them over to one of my colleagues, who would sit down with Vydec and produce an almost-readable manuscript. Which I would proof, she would rerevise, and together we would present to Tiger as if it were our gift to him.

Tiger, it seemed, had as much trouble grasping the concept of a word processor as I had with the concept of a marble boat. He just couldn't make it float in his head. And so every time we gave him a neat new manuscript to review—and even after we'd let him stand near Vydec and watch as words were typed and came up on the screen and as pages with those very words were spit out of the printer—he'd go all the way back to the drawing board and spend days mistyping his next revision. Which he would deliver to me, smiling broadly. And we'd start all over again. If any of those papers ever got published, it was after he returned to China, and probably in his own language.

I've kept the little piece of silk with the marble boat—in a plain white ceramic frame—near at hand for all the years since I knew Tiger John. It's a reminder of people I met in that hospital half a lifetime ago, people from across the country and around the globe. It's also been a reminder that what seems impossible often can be done. I mean, if ancient Chinese engineers could figure out how to make a marble boat float, anything is possible, right?

Except that's not exactly what happened. Not long ago while cleaning up my home office (a highly effective tactic for avoiding the work of revision), I dusted the frame around my silk marble boat and thought to myself, I should Google that. And I did, and discovered that while there is indeed such a structure on the grounds of the

Summer Palace in Beijing, originally built in 1755, it is a lakeside pavilion shaped like a boat, not a vessel that was ever meant to float. The Marble Boat is sometimes called the Boat of Purity and Ease, which is what one can only aspire to when it comes to writing—and revision.

So lately, I've been thinking about the marble boat in a whole new way. I've been using it as a reminder that Tiger John made revision so much harder than it had to be. Like I do, but in a different way. Because when I do finally get around to rereading myself, I almost always find some things to like about what I've written, even when I also see ways it could be improved. And so I sit with my pages and start marking them up, and eventually I head for my computer, open the file, and begin revising in earnest. Perhaps not with purity and ease, but with every intention of making the work better, making it sing, maybe even making it sail.

Prevailing Wind, Ballycastle • ink on paper

When the Bough . . .

. . . Breaks

EARLY MARCH AND A NOR'EASTER IS HOWLING, DUMPING snow, felling trees, snapping wires. The wires spark dazzling electrical fires that dance across the sidewalk, blaze into the street, and summon firefighters who yell through megaphones at my neighbors and me to stay inside. In the swirl of the storm and the dark of a power outage (which will last four days), I don't notice the broken limb on a tree behind my house until morning. It hangs from the treetop like an arm fractured at the elbow—an arm long enough to reach from my second-floor bedroom window to the lawn, with hundreds of skinny branches fingering the snowy surface below.

. . . Buds

Late April, my little corner of the world is still recovering from that first, worst storm and three other snowy nor'easters that followed in rapid succession, none of which has coaxed the broken bough to earth. How, I wonder, have thousands of feathery green baby buds missed the memo announcing the demise of this particular branch? How can they still be drawing sustenance across the splintered wood I can see from my attic? With my trusty orange clippers and a handsaw, I hack away at lower branches until my gloved fingers blister. Then I collect the branches, cradle them in my weary arms, ferry them to trash bins in the garage, then drag those to the curb. Now that the massive limb is no longer propped up by parts wedged into the muddy earth, I can wiggle it, like a loose tooth. A loose tooth that is not yet ready to yield to external pressure, but will take its own sweet time.

...Blossoms

Mid-May, and everything else is in full bloom, so why not? The branches I couldn't reach with my tools are in full-on leaf mode, the lanky limb is now wearing a fluttery, bright green skirt. I laugh along with Mother Nature. I learn to duck around this dangling obstacle as I mow the lawn. I wonder what the neighbors think, not that many of them can see my leafy broken bough, but still. It's far enough from the back of the house and the side of the garage that it can't break a window or land on a roof when it falls. When the wind blows, I watch from a window, wondering. Wiggling gives way to rocking, and I can sense the stubborn sinew above is softening. But for now, this tree toys with me more than I with it.

...Browns

In the blistering heat of July, I bristle. Ugly, rust-colored leaves taunt me each time I step out the back door or glance out the window. I pull a workbench close to the bough, climb up with my clippers and saw, go after the now-brittle branches with a vengeance. After, I take to swinging the branch back and forth, even swirling it in wide circles, whenever I pass through the yard; whenever, that is, I pass through the yard and no one else is within sight or earshot. As I swing and swirl the limb I hum—sometimes in my head, sometimes aloud, but softly—"Rock-a-Bye, Baby." I Google the lyrics to that troubling little ditty. Then I Google the phrase "Mexican standoff," which seems to apply. I swing. I swirl. I hum, most often in double-time.

...Bellyflops

At long last, over Labor Day weekend. For nearly two weeks I've ignored that unsightly, fractured limb. One hot afternoon, I sneak up on it, grab it with both hands, and send it swirling into the air. The creaking overhead sounds different, looser than before. I step back and watch as the bough breaks free in mid-swing, grazes the holly bushes, clatters to the ground, then rolls over until it's reclining on one elbow-like branch that's made a deep divot in the grass. Dangling, it looked like a plumb line, and I imagined it would spear its way into the soil. But supine, it's the crookedest big old stick I've ever seen. Once more I wield my tree-trimming tools, amputating bits that stick out, some as thick as my wrist. When no one is looking, I wrestle what's left of the broken bough into the underbrush where a line of trees and shrubs separates my yard from the next. I feel almost like I'm hiding a body. I wonder, will I ever walk through my yard again without hearing that creepy lullaby in my head?

Van Morrison and Me

> *Sometimes I wonder if I inadvertently postponed my own writing life because I'd fallen in love with other people's words, and I'd let that be enough.*

IT'S BEEN A WHILE SINCE I RAN OUT AND BOUGHT A CD ON the day it was released. Not because I buy music online and download it onto something that plugs into my ears. I don't. In fact, I don't own a single device that comes with earbuds, or whatever the kids call those things these days. It's just that I already have so many CDs that I'm pretty selective about acquiring new ones.

But I've been waiting for the new release from Van Morrison for a few months, ever since I heard its title—"Born to Sing: No Plan B." Those words got into my head and got me thinking about the confidence it would take to substitute "write" for "sing" and claim that as my mantra. Writing always was my Plan A. Anything else I've ever done on the way to becoming a writer, I stumbled into more than sought out, thereby proving—if you follow my logic—that I never had a Plan B.

So here I sit, listening to the ten songs on the new album (his thirty-fifth!) for the third time in as many days. "Born to Sing" isn't even my favorite track. I mean it's still Van Morrison warbling and doing that thing he does with his saxophone, making me sway and swoon over my keyboard and around my house. It's that idea of "No Plan B" I'm stuck on. I can't help wondering how long he's felt that way—since before his first album? Or maybe after his tenth?

"No Plan B means this is not a rehearsal," Van explains in

the liner notes. "That's the main thing—it's not a hobby, it's real, happening now in real time."

By that definition, I am indeed working my Plan A—in the odd hours outside the day jobs I've held since leaving the corporate world—first in my favorite theater company, then in a nonprofit arts agency, now in the student writing center of a health sciences university. These are the jobs that pay the bills. And they are jobs I've really liked, mind you. The first two because they brought me into daily contact with other people who have given themselves over entirely to their art-making. The third because I am helping people learn how to write, how to tell their stories, how to express themselves, and how to contribute to medical knowledge by communicating clearly. I take paid vacations to go away and write. I write on weekends, I write in the evenings, I scribble notes to myself on the train, I squeeze in courses and workshops whenever I can.

I've never thought of writing as a hobby. It's real, all right; it's one of the real-est parts of me. So what if I was nearly fifty before Plan A kicked in and my writing life began in earnest? Sometimes I wonder if I inadvertently postponed my own writing life because I'd fallen in love with other people's words, and I'd let that be enough. Other literary authors, of course. But singer-songwriters too. Like Joan Baez. Like Mary-Chapin Carpenter. Like Dar Williams. Like Van Morrison.

When it comes to my own writing, there's no turning back now, I'm certain of that.

And yet, I still have my doubts about my degree of certainty. Would I, if I could, give myself over entirely to my writing? Some days I think yes, other days I take a long walk or turn to my garden to see what answer I might unearth there.

In "Born to Sing," Van attributes his art to passion, not reason. Does my passion for writing run that deep, does it spring from a "sense of absolute conviction" (again, the liner notes)? Or is it fueled by a sense of urgency because I have to fit it in around the margins of my other life?

Of course, Van Morrison has been making music forever. He's allowed to exude utter confidence, and he's got the resume to back up his claim that he never had (or needed) a Plan B. And clearly, he doesn't have to worry about a day job.

Dear Santa Fe

> *Did I mention Denise and I were visiting you, in part, to celebrate our recent sixtieth birthdays?*

DEAR SANTA FE,

I've just returned from a nearly perfect week-long sojourn in you. For the record, my fist visit was in 2006, and this was my seventh trip to you, so please believe I am writing because of my deep affection and my sincere intention to return at the first opportunity, if only you can once again make your streets safe for people like me.

On the first evening of my recent visit, after more than twelve tiring hours of travel from my home near Philadelphia, which required a 4:00 am start; after my friend Denise, who traveled from DC, and I rendezvoused in Albuquerque, drove north under a steely sky streaked with lightning; hauled our luggage up forty-one steps from the parking lot to a rented condo; unpacked (another sixteen steps up to the bedrooms) and wandered into town for an early dinner; and after we groggily started strolling back toward the condo in light drizzle, at last relaxing into the mellow vibe of you, we had our first encounter with one of those thin little aliens who has invaded your otherwise charming downtown since our last visit, three years ago.

This first encounter was by far the most memorable—as you shall hear—but in the days that followed I would realize that, except for her French accent (which may or may not have been authentic) and her white lab coat (or did my mind invent that?), our first alien was cut from the same strange cloth as her pushy little alien friends.

We were walking along the Old Santa Fe Trail, just opposite La Fonda, when a pretty young brunette with a convincing French accent materialized from the doorframe of an eerily bright, shiny little shop that was not there in 2016. She swiftly handed us each a small packet of face moisturizer, although at the time we didn't even know what we'd been handed. We just thanked her and kept walking. In a flash, she popped back into her little shop, then popped back out onto the sidewalk, and started chasing us down the street waving a thick syringe in her dainty, possibly French, hand, wearing (I am certain of it now!) a white lab coat, bright red lipstick, and black stilettos. She said something about stem cells and helping us get rid of our "lines." Over my shoulder, as we quickened our pace to escape the looming syringe, I shouted back to her, "I've earned my lines, thank you very much." That stopped her in her petite tracks, or more likely, sent her scuttling back to the shop to reload her palm with more free samples of moisturizer. The night was still young; the tourists were only just beginning to swarm.

The next day, refreshed and ready to reacquaint myself with favorite sights and stops around you—while Denise went off to climb a mountain—I was surprised when a lanky young man posed ever-so-carefully at the portal to a clothing store on East San Francisco Street suddenly came to life and handed me—no, forced into my hand—another small white packet of face cream. I thanked him and kept moving, even as he tried to stop me with an offer of something for my eyes. "You might like it," he shouted, in a tone more sinister than seductive.

Later, as I walked along Water Street, I spotted another waifish young man lingering in a now-familiar pose in the doorway of a jewelry shop—not an establishment that might be expected to trade in skin-care products—and I knew even before I reached him that he, too, would try to press a small white pouch of something into my hand. But by now I was onto this game. I quickened my steps. I edged toward the curb and dodged his unfurling arm. I ignored his offer of cream for my neck. As I blew past, he exhaled a bit angrily, as if *he* were the one being accosted at every turn by aggressive little mannequins intent on applying their unsolicited products to *his* skin!

Did I mention Denise and I were visiting you, in part, to celebrate our recent sixtieth birthdays? (Okay, we'll both turn sixty-one in a matter of weeks, but it's been a challenging year—although not dermatologically speaking.) No doubt we each have acquired some "lines" in the thirty-plus years we've been friends. But we don't have noticeably more lines than we did three years ago. So what is up with these insulting, ubiquitous free samples, aimed squarely at female visitors of a certain vintage?

The behavior exhibited by this small army of doorway lurkers—I've described three, but trust me, there were others—is, in my opinion, the opposite of what I've come to expect from the friendly, welcoming Santa Feans I've met on previous visits. Frankly, I'm not sure they add value in a town like you that relies so heavily on tourism. Furthermore, I've always been struck with the casual elegance and natural looks of Santa Fe women; every time I visit you I vow to stop coloring my hair and let it go silver like they do. (This time I lasted a whole three weeks before I cracked.) I've come to understand that one part of your appeal—not even almost the largest part, which is how you always feed my creative self and top up my tank of happy—is a chance to observe so many gracefully aging women in one place. I'm not naive; I'm sure they all use skin-care products. But in the privacy of their own *casitas*, not right out there on the Plaza, dispensed from fat syringes being wielded by oh-so-thin twenty-somethings who have been trained to never, ever utter the word "wrinkle."

Here's what I want to know, my dear Santa Fe: Who sent these moisturizer-pushing creatures to invade you? Did they misread their instructions and perhaps arrive in New Mexico, the Land of *Enchantment*, when they were meant to go to the Land of *Enhancement*, maybe California, say, or Florida? (I can tell you, they wouldn't last ten minutes in Philly.) Did they just drift northward from Roswell? Have you given them permission to be there? If so, you ought to rethink that decision. If you want to offer free samples to tourists, consider less judge-y products. I, for example, would happily accept dark chocolate and/or mango salsa; better yet, sangria, or even turquoise nuggets.

By the way, that first free sample, the one from the possibly French alien, was made in Amsterdam and "infused with grape stem cell extract." Who even knew grapes had stem cells? I did not. But while that one-tenth-of-one-ounce packet and the one other I collected—from Hawaii, made with white truffle extract—both remain unopened, there is still an excellent chance I managed to infuse my skin with grape stem cells while I was visiting you.

Denise and I spent a thoroughly pleasant hour or so in the Gruet Winery Santa Fe Tasting Room—also new since our last visit—sampling some gorgeous local bubbly. My face, eyes, and neck felt better almost instantly.

Yours in holy faith,
Eileen

Express Train • acrylic on paper

Special Delivery

> *It was (almost) common courtesy. It had (almost)
> nothing to do with that long-ago sisters' weekend
> when Amy had shortsheeted the beds.*

W**E'VE ALL BEEN THERE, RIGHT?** Y**OU'VE JUST STEPPED OUT** of the shower, there's a great song on the radio, and no one else is home. Of course you're going to sing along, maybe even do a little dance as you towel off and comb your wet hair. Your husband's at work, your kids are at school, and you feel like letting go just a little. In fact, maybe you're going to keep on singing and dancing even as you leave the bathroom and wander—no longer wrapped in a towel—into the bedroom, and wriggle into your black big-girl panties (think *Bridget Jones's Diary*) and your best black bra. And let's say maybe, just maybe, you're going to sing so loudly that your singing drowns out the sound of a FedEx delivery truck making its way down your long, steep driveway and coming to a stop directly outside your first-floor bedroom window, where the shade is up to let the May sunshine in because nobody, but nobody, ever drives down that long, steep hill unexpectedly.

Let's say the only eye contact you make with the FedEx driver—although you will sign for the package he is there to deliver—is through that window, while you are still mostly undressed. He is so close to you—simply by virtue of where he has parked his truck—that there is no denying he has seen you. You cannot pretend no one is home, and neither can he. So you lock eyes, ever so briefly, in spite of yourselves. And then all you can do, while he fumbles for his clipboard, double-checks the address, and noisily slides open the door of his truck to find your package, is drop to the floor, roll toward your closet, and start grabbing at the hems of clothes. You are hoping to find something modest, like maybe a thick turtleneck sweater and your baggiest sweatpants. When the doorbell rings, you somehow have the presence of mind to turn down the volume on the radio and then walk, as calmly as you can—which is not very calmly at all—to the front door, suppressing an urge to trill, "Who is it?" as you reluctantly reach for the doorknob.

What would you do with this story, if it happened to you?

Well, if you were my sister Amy, you would manage, sort of, to keep your composure as you signed for that package, without ever looking directly at the delivery man. Then you would go back into your bedroom, pull all the shades all the way down, and collapse onto your bed in a ridiculous heap of mortified laughter. After a few minutes, you would take off the clothes you'd scrambled into, go back into the bathroom to generously reapply deodorant, and then put on the clothes you had intended to wear that morning—a dark ensemble, since you were heading to a funeral, which explains the black undergarments. (The funeral is not for someone you were close to, as should be obvious, but for the husband of your son's schoolbus driver.)

And then you would pause for a moment and think to yourself, "Thank goodness we have a girls' weekend planned. I can't wait to tell my sisters and my mother *this* story."

We did indeed have a girls' weekend planned, shortly after Amy's close encounter with the FedEx driver. Our sister Angie was turning fifty, and along with Mom, Amy's twin sister, Jen, me, and a couple of Angie's close friends, we were driving to Amy's home—a mountain retreat in Maryland—to celebrate. Amy's husband was taking the kids to visit his parents that weekend (wise man), so we had the whole lovely house to ourselves, and with a couple of extra air mattresses, way too much food, and assorted adult beverages, we were set for some fun. And fun we had, especially after Amy told us her FedEx story on the first night we were there. We laughed ourselves silly, just imagining what she'd been through and how she'd felt.

But the best fun came in the days following our girls' weekend. Because on the way home, Jen and I cooked up a wicked plan while Angie and Mom dozed in the backseat. We decided that we would each have to—just to be polite—send Amy thank-you notes for being such a wonderful hostess. It was (almost) common courtesy. It had (almost) nothing to do with that long-ago sisters' weekend, when Amy had arrived first, checked in for all of us, and short-sheeted the beds in the room Jen and I were sharing.

On the following Tuesday morning, when someone unexpectedly rang Amy's doorbell, she thought it was very funny that I'd sent her a thank-you note, via FedEx.

On Wednesday, she began to sense a pattern when she got a note from Jen, again delivered by FedEx. The driver—who was never the same one who'd made that first delivery, who apparently had asked for a new route, perhaps in another state—asked if they were buying a house or something, with so much overnight mail. Amy just shook her head and answered, "No, that's not it."

By Thursday she was ready. Mom's thank-you note and Angie's arrived together, and Amy laughed and laughed when she heard that at the Mail Boxes Etc. store, Angie had been told there were, in fact, cheaper options available for overnight shipping. But she had insisted on using Federal Express.

The Writing on the Wall

A ripple of surprise went around the table. A look of vindication washed across Angie's face, while Mom looked shocked, then sheepish.

WHAT I REMEMBER, AS IF IT HAPPENED YESTERDAY, NOT more than fifty years ago, is this: eavesdropping from the top of the basement stairs as my sister Angie was being scolded for writing her name on the wall in letters that were about a foot tall, using black shoe polish, the kind that comes in a bottle with a wide sponge applicator. At first, I was sure I'd be caught, now that my days' old handiwork had been discovered by Pop-Pop and reported to Mom. But after Angie was summoned to the basement of our still-new home and denied having anything to do with the graffiti on the unfinished cinder block, I could sense my plan was working.

"I didn't do it," Angie wailed.

"Don't make it worse by lying," Mom replied.

"But I *didn't*," she insisted.

What I can't recall, no matter how hard I try, is this: what exactly Angie had done to provoke me to scrawl those letters on the wall, hoping she would be blamed. I know for certain this wasn't a random act of sibling mischief; I was really mad at her for something and determined to get even. But what? What could she have done to me—she was only four or five years old and I was only six or seven—to have inspired such a spiteful act?

"Of course you did it, Angela. We know it was you. Who else would have written your name that way, with the 'N' backwards?"

Um, maybe the person who had been working with her for

weeks, teaching her how to write her name on the small chalkboard in the basement, trying and trying to help her master her Ns? Maybe she did it?

But no one went there. No one would have suspected good little me of such a dastardly act. Even I found it hard to believe I'd done it. And even harder to believe I'd gotten away with it.

Angie got in trouble—not too much, I think. She was probably made to sit under the desk in the kitchen for ten minutes. In our house "under the desk" was what today would be called "a time out." The desk was a built-in counter between two cabinets, not the worst place to sit—although it became less comfortable as one grew—but it served its purpose as a place for cooling off and contemplating punishable behaviors. Maybe Mom hadn't even invented "under the desk" yet at the time of the shoe polish caper, maybe all that happened to Angie was that scolding in the basement. Still, I felt the powerful itch I'd had to seek revenge had been scratched. And Mom was pretty certain Angie would never write her name on that wall again, in shoe polish or any other medium.

I've often wondered: What did Angie's little-girl brain do with that experience? Even she didn't think to blame me, and surely she knew—at least when her name was first discovered—that she had not put it there. Was it a lingering mystery in her mind? Did she ever doubt her own innocence? It wasn't something we talked about then, or for a long time afterward. Although for all of our growing-up years, we spent a little time in that basement almost every Sunday evening, polishing our Catholic-school saddle shoes on old sheets of newspaper, sponging on white as well as black or blue liquid, letting it dry, then buffing each shoe so we'd start the week in clean-looking (if unstylish) footwear.

I was thirty-something when I finally confessed to writing Angie's name on that wall. A bunch of us were gathered around the kitchen table, my parents and some combination of the seven siblings, maybe an in-law or two. I don't remember how the topic came up—bad things we'd done as kids, ways we'd gotten each other in trouble, or perhaps a funny story about something one of my then-little nieces or nephews had done to torture a sibling. Somebody mentioned Angie's name on the basement wall—a wall that had since been painted more than once—and without hesitating, I'd volunteered, "Oh, I did that."

A ripple of surprise went around the table. A look of vindication washed across Angie's face, while Mom looked shocked, then sheepish. I felt relieved to say it out loud, at last. I mean, what was going to happen now? We were all adults, and the statute of limitations on my perfect crime had long since expired. We had a good laugh and went back to whatever else we'd been talking about. But the truth about that long-ago episode was now indelibly written into our family lore, in thick, wet letters. An event that had been buried for decades had resurfaced, and from then on, references to shoe polish and backward Ns peppered family conversations and got woven into the punchlines for other stories.

Just this spring, my siblings and I spent a lot of time clearing out the considerable contents of that same basement in the house where our parents had lived for fifty-five years, the house we have always thought of as home, wherever else each of us has lived. Last December, we helped Mom and Dad move into an apartment in a nearby senior community, where they are now happily settled. Before they moved, we had several rounds with Mom of going through family treasures and watching her hand them off to kids and grandkids. Even after they moved, Mom and Dad came back several times as we sorted through closets or showed them what we'd done to get the house ready to sell. But the work of emptying out the basement—and everything else in the house that didn't fit in the apartment or hadn't been claimed by one of us—fell to the siblings and our families. It was a true team effort, one that evoked many happy memories, and about equal amounts of laughter, tears, and sweat; and more text messages and photographs than I could count.

A bunch of us spent an entire day in late March hauling furniture and other items that were beyond repair up the cellar steps and into a dumpster in the driveway. We filled that dumpster to the brim, although there were still lots of usable items in the basement to be divvied up or donated. We couldn't believe how big the space looked when we were done that day—big enough that we older siblings could recall how it felt to roller skate down there when the house was new and the basement felt like an indoor playground; or how we'd put on shows with our cousins or the dozens of kids who'd lived on our block back then; or how much time we'd spent playing ping-pong or torturing our Uncle Mickey while he sat at a big wooden desk wearing earphones and studied for law school.

And of course, a day spent in that basement could not pass without a few references to Angie's name being written on the wall in black shoe polish by her twisted sister. Good times.

Once we'd mostly emptied the basement, it was obvious the walls and floor would need to be painted before the house went on the market. Crammed shelves around the perimeter and assorted desks, tables, and other furniture had masked the dingy surfaces. We hired a painter to make the old basement look more presentable. Then we set about decluttering the two upstairs floors, getting our happy old house ready to become a real estate listing for the first time in its history. Three weeks after it went on the market, we had an offer. And then it was time for the final round of clearing out, and saying goodbye to the house, which we did one at a time—sometimes alone, sometimes with spouses and kids—over the last two weeks before settlement.

Dennis drove away for the last time first, with Mom and Dad in the car, after he'd spent most of a Sunday dragging big stuff down the stairs and out to the driveway; he'd even gone into the attic to dig out the original, now-crumbling playpen, a relic as old as me. Brian checked out the following Friday, after he and Amy dragged more big stuff to the curb; his car was loaded with some of Mom's artwork, which he was taking home to store. Pete left on Saturday, after a bunch of us made some Goodwill runs. Amy (crying like a baby, as she texted) and her family left later that day, after her daughter Samantha had taken most of the remaining furniture to her new apartment. Jen and her family stopped by for the last time on Sunday, to collect the remaining tools from the basement and donate them to a nonprofit where she used to work.

So in the final days, it came down to me and Angie, the two oldest and the two nearest, geographically, to clear out the few remaining items. Settlement was Friday. Angie went Monday night to put out the trash one last time. I collected some things Tuesday, then went to the house for what I thought would be the last time Wednesday, to meet a man who was picking up the living room rug. Angie would stop by Thursday night to pick up the two lamps on timers that we'd left in the front windows for the last six months.

We all knew we were running out of days to call that house "home," and we were doing all we could to keep each other focused on happy stuff. So after the rug guy left, I put myself under the desk for one last time and (once the tears stopped) I took a rare selfie to send to my siblings. I got a few LOLs as well as kudos for being able to get myself into—and out of—that tight space at my age. I made one last pass through every room in the house, then I got into my car and pulled out of the driveway, tears streaming down my face. That evening, Angie sent a group text saying she might just write her name on the basement wall Thursday night. "With shoe polish?" I asked. She said she hadn't decided.

Thursday happened to be Angie's birthday. So I got her one extra little present, even though it meant I had to say goodbye to the house all over again. Beside the lamp in the living room, I left a note that said, "Happy Birthday, Angie. You get the last word." Along with, of course, a bottle of black shoe polish. That day, I smiled as I pulled out of the driveway. My parents laughed and laughed when I told them what I'd done.

Late that night, after Angie and her husband and son had collected the lamps and said their own teary farewells to the house, she texted us two pictures. One showed her writing her name (not mine, which might have been even funnier) on the basement wall—with a pen, not shoe polish, although she said that was the best birthday present ever—in letters that were only a few inches high; a close-up showed her backwards N. It's in a spot covered by one of the shelves we left behind for the new owners, so they might not see it right away.

Still, we all know it's there, and it feels good knowing that the writing (writing that represents the insidest of inside jokes) is on a wall where so much laughter bounced off those cinder blocks over the decades, as it did on every wall in that well-loved, much-missed house.

Down Came a Blackbird • acrylic and collage on canvas

The Sound of a Flinch

Why, I wonder, can these birds remember exactly which house and exactly which hanging basket to nest in, but look at me every time—through that one unflinching, glassy black bead—as if I am a brand-new threat, not an accommodating (if reluctant) landlady?

IF THE TERM "BEADY-EYED" WAS NOT COINED IN REFERENCE to the mourning dove, it ought to have been. I've had ample time to assess the shiny black eyeballs of these pretty birds over the last several summers, since a pair (maybe pairs?) of them determined that a hanging flower basket just outside my back door is the perfect spot for nesting. Again and again. And then some more.

I only ever see one beady eye at a time because the birds always position themselves parallel to the door, although not always facing the same direction. Seen in profile, I can appreciate their delicately shaped heads and the sharp black beaks that curve downward ever so slightly. I love, love, love the cocoa-powder brown of their feathers, flecked with soft black spots. I love the way they sometimes collapse their small heads deep into their bodies as they guard their precious eggs. I even love their plaintive four-note call, the reason the doves are described as "mourning"; I recognized this distinctive element of my local soundscape long before the birds took up residence in my flower basket, although I've noticed they never sound these notes while nesting.

Here's what I don't love: having a brightly colored flowering plant purchased from my favorite nursery wither and die because I cannot water it while the doves are nesting. Having my back door—

the easiest access to my herb garden, my detached garage, and my hose and watering can—commandeered for weeks, even months, at a time. Having to dispose of those weeks'/months' worth of accumulated bird droppings and sticky fragments of eggshell at the end of each summer. Having to replace the fiber liner in my wire hanging basket every spring. Never so much as a thank-you note left behind and no way to withhold an unmade security deposit to cover the damages.

And what I most especially don't love is the way the doves make me flinch—over and over again—sometimes just because I've opened the storm door to let fresh air into the kitchen, other times because I've dared to crack open the screen door and tiptoe down my back steps. *My* back steps.

It's a mutual flinch, I know, and on both sides it's instinctual. We startle each other, almost every time. Typically, it's a six-part movement: the click of the lock on the heavy storm door, the metallic ping of the lock on the wood-framed screen door, the rub of the door against its jamb (especially on steamy summer days) as I gently ease it open. And then, a flash of brown feathers and a low-level squeal as the bird takes flight, accompanied one-half beat later by a low-level shriek from me and a rocking motion as the long basket swings on its hook. I've come to think of this sequence as the sound of a flinch.

Some of what I know about mourning doves I've learned from my mother. The first summer they moved into my flower basket, Mom was recovering—oh-so-slowly—from a series of medical challenges that had kept her in the hospital and then in a rehab facility for nearly six months. I'd tell her about the doves when I'd visit with her, knowing she sorely missed the view of trees and birds from her own kitchen window and felt deprived of her webcam obsession with an eagles' nest and the daily drama of waiting for those far-away eggs to hatch. She's the one who told me that male and female mourning doves take turns minding a nest. She thought it was funny that they startled me so often and that I resented having my back porch taken over by birds; she would have loved such close viewing and such intimate encounters. As I gave Mom updates and saw her take great pleasure in them, my stance toward the doves softened. By the time those first eggs had been hatched and the babies had morphed into squabs, they'd kind of won me over. I did enjoy watching the little family through my screen door, or more stealthily from my dining room window. I witnessed voice lessons—that four-note call *sotto voce*—and even flying lessons. I was nearly as proud as the parent birds when those babies flew my coop.

Until I saw what they'd left behind in the ruined basket liner. Yuck. I made a mental note to buy some netting the following spring, to make it clear that my flower basket was not accepting tenants and was not available for use as a birdy birthing center and latrine.

But by fall, when I should have been tucking that basket and others away in my garage, I was preoccupied with the emptying out of a different nest. Mom's health was improving, but after what she'd been through, and with Dad having developed new health challenges, too, my six siblings and I were preparing to help my parents move out of the house they'd lived in for fifty-five years and into an apartment. I managed to rake the leaves in my yard, but forgot all about the hanging baskets and so many other tasks I've come to think of as putting my garden to bed for the winter. The nest where we'd all been fledged as young humans needed clearing out and sprucing up—and yes, a bit of mourning—so we could sell it. All my energy was wrapped up in that effort from early fall well into the beginning of the next summer. Through a winter of wicked nor'easters, I watched snow pile up in the three flower baskets on my back porch. Then, before I even had a chance to think about buying annuals for my garden or netting for my best hanging basket, the doves had moved back in and were settled comfortably around the skeletal remains of an ornamental pepper I'd planted at the end of the previous summer. A new season of nesting and flinching and fledging and making a filthy mess was well underway.

Gentle reader, this feels like the right moment to let you know that since I moved into my house more than 20 summers ago, I have always had bird houses scattered around my property. They've hung from the tree in my front yard, perched beneath my living room window, dangled from the back fence, and swayed from poles placed among the shrubbery. I'm always thrilled to see twigs poking out from the openings of these small abodes or to observe rocking motions that let me know some birdy has accepted my invitation to move in. I thrill at the birdsong that greets me every morning, beginning in early spring, and I mourn its lapse during the colder months. I hope you will keep this in mind when I tell you that after two years of having my back porch invaded and the floral selections for my favorite basket ruined, I decided the following spring to make it clear to the mourning doves that they should find somewhere else to nest.

I bought a pretty purple plant for my hanging basket. Then I took the remnants of a broken old wind chime—one made from mismatched pieces of silverware—and tucked those pointy objects around the outer edge of the flowers. It was a not-so-subtle sign that clearly read "Keep Out." And it worked. Or so I thought. Until the final weekend in July, when in the throes of a nasty heatwave, I noticed some twiggy debris on my back porch as I approached the steps. Then suddenly, a tawny flash, that odd little squeal, and me, caught off guard, once again emitting my own half shriek/half gasp.

The sound of a flinch when I had at last stopped expecting it.

And so began our third season of scaring the feathers off each other on an almost daily basis, me and my mourning doves. I was intrigued by their ability to take off and land around the pointy utensils in the nest, although I noticed one fork had been nudged into a new position. I didn't dare reach into the nest to remove the erstwhile utensils for fear of further aggravating the situation. Mom was oh-so-happy to hear that the mourning doves had returned to my flower basket. She was even happier with their pluckiness after I told her what I'd done to try to keep them out—although she in no way approved of my defensive ploy. She eagerly awaited news of the soon-to-be hatchlings.

After that season of nesting, I removed the remnants of that old windchime, along with the soiled basket liner, and accepted my seasonal birdy boarders as a fact of life. Now, several cycles of fledging later, I have no way of knowing if it's the same pair of doves nesting in my basket every time. But in addition to what Mom told me, I've done a little research. I've learned these birds like to nest under eaves or in other partially sheltered spots, and that once they find a nesting place they like, they are inclined to return, as many as five times in a single mating season. Each time they nest—typically with two eggs—the male and female take turns incubating, just as Mom explained; for about two weeks, he takes the day shift, she takes the night shift, with one or the other constantly on duty. I've never seen the changing of the guard, but the birds are so similar in size it appears as though the same creature sits in stony silence all day and all night—except, of course, when I get too close and s/he hits the ejector button and temporarily flashes off to the peak of my garage roof, where I swear s/he gives me a beady-eyed dirty look.

Once the eggs hatch, the mama and papa continue to share parenting duties for another two weeks or so as their fledglings develop. Those are the weeks I don't even think about using my back steps, because the adult birds are on red alert against intruders. Why, I wonder, can these birds remember exactly which house and exactly which hanging basket to nest in, but look at me every time—through that one unflinching, glassy black bead—as if I am a brand-new threat, not an accommodating (if reluctant) landlady? Why can't they just let me slide past the nest, walk down three steps, take out the trash or collect a handful of basil from the garden, then slip back through the door without getting their feathers ruffled? Don't they see how I check on them after every thunderstorm or how I shooed those big, noisy crows out of the yard just the other day? Do they not appreciate my efforts to quietly remove a screen in an upstairs window so I can take pictures of their thumb-sized babies to share with Mom?

I read online recently that what I've thought of as a squeal—the sound of a mourning dove launching into flight (from anywhere, not just from my hanging basket full of dead flowers)—is a sound made by the bird's wings, not a gasp of surprise from its breast, like the one it elicits from mine. In its own way, this new information startles me, making me feel more skittish than the birds. The sound made by their wings is described as "a sharp whistling or whinnying." But to me, it is, and will remain, from one mating season to the next, the sound of a flinch.

Chez Nous • acrylic on paper

Happy Hour

If someone had a friend join us for dinner—which happened often enough—we all squished in a little closer, with those at the ends of the bench at serious risk of losing their perches.

Clingety-clang. Clangety-cling.

THE OLD DINNER BELL RANG OUT THROUGH THE neighborhood, calling our scattered tribe home to the brick house in the middle of the block, the house labeled "441." Mounted on the wall at the top of the back-door steps, the black iron bell would have been rung by Mom—or whomever she'd tagged to ring it for her that day. In our suburban street full of large families and seemingly endless games of hide-and-seek and wiffle ball, in that long-ago era when we made our own playdates (although we most certainly did not call them that), most of the year we played outside after school for as long as we could, weather and schoolwork permitting. In summer, some days we left the house after breakfast, maybe popped in for lunch or to change into or out of a bathing suit, and didn't come home again until the dinner bell insisted we must.

Most of my siblings showed up with the first sounding of the bell. We older ones might have been finishing homework or helping with dinner, while the younger ones were corralled inside the redwood-stained fence that defined our back yard. Dennis often needed a second or third call, and sometimes someone had to be sent out looking for him. He always was the most likely to have strayed beyond earshot of the bell; also the most likely to be eating his "first dinner" in someone else's kitchen before he slid into place on one of the long, padded picnic benches that flanked our kitchen table—the better to accommodate Mom and the seven kids. Dad and our grandfather co-anchored the table's ends.

If someone showed up with their after-school shirt worn inside out, it meant she or he had gotten 100 on a test.

If a brother got up to get a second glass of milk (or more likely, a towel for one he'd just knocked over) or otherwise found an excuse to walk around the table while we ate, a sister almost certainly got goosed along the way, causing at least a shriek and a vertical lift off her seat, and often a ripple effect all along the crowded bench.

If a brother timed a punchline or a jab just so, another brother might be made to exhale milk and maybe even a few fragments of partially masticated dinner through his nose.

If someone had a friend join us for dinner—which happened often enough—we all squished in a little closer, with those at the ends of the bench at serious risk of losing their perches. Occasionally, someone did slip off an end and land on the floor. Sometimes, it was an accident.

There was plenty of chattering—although not maybe as much as you would expect, at least while we ate our "firsts." We all knew that if you wanted seconds, especially on mashed potatoes, you had to clean your plate quickly and reach for the bowl before others beat you to it. The conversation always picked up once the serving bowls were empty.

At least until dessert was served, and "firsts" began all over again.

We never called dinner time "happy hour." No adult beverages were involved, although my parents might occasionally each sip a small glass of wine before dinner, after Dad got home from work and while Mom was cooking.

But oh, those dinnertime hours were some of the happiest happy hours I have lived through on this planet—despite (and also because of) sibling shenanigans, parental warnings, grandfatherly glares, buckets of spilled milk, enough mashed potatoes that everyone almost always had enough, and a never-ending cacophony of sneezes, burps, and giggles, occasionally interrupted by the phone or the doorbell.

Over time, of course, one by one we moved away from every-night meals at that kitchen table, a table that to the best of my recollection was only ever replaced one time in the fifty-five years we called that house home.

At some point during the nest-emptying years, which, it should be noted, began almost four decades ago, in honor of our street address—that magical number we've all come to love—we started calling ourselves "Club 441." We even had a flag made with that name, to hang from the front porch flagpole on days when we gathered there.

When my parents moved last year to an apartment, the (second) old kitchen table moved into my niece Samantha's first post-college apartment. In theory, we could all still gather around it, but we'd have to eat in shifts, since there are now more than thirty of us, including a fledgling second-generation of in-laws and one great-grandchild.

Blinkety-blink. Strummety-strum.

My telephone beckons, its little blue light flashing at me, the gentle ring tone called "harp glissando" letting me know a text message has been delivered.

If it happens at the right time of day, it puts me in mind of the old dinner bell, and it makes me hope one of my siblings is on the other end of that little blue blinkety-blink.

As often as not, one of them is. At first. Then two or three or four or six more of them chime in. And in no time at all a virtual meeting of Club 441 is underway.

Maybe I'm already in my kitchen making dinner. Maybe I'm on the train coming home from the city. Or maybe, like that one Friday last August, I'm at a writing conference, literally heading for a scheduled happy hour when my purse starts buzzing.

Dennis: Happy hour in Hampton Roads, visitors welcome. [Plus photo of deck chairs and the bay outside his door, framed by an oh-so-blue sky]

Brian: Now you tell me! [Hampton Roads is a five-hour drive from where he is, having spent the day shuttling Mom and Dad to medical appointments]

Angie: Looks lovely! Happy hour in Ocean City, NJ. [Plus photo of empty beach, with countless footprints in the sand, as if everyone has just scurried off to a nearby bar]

Pete: Happy Hour in Empty Nest, PA. [Plus photo of back patio with four empty chairs, since he's just dropped his youngest off at college for her first semester]

Amy: [Photo from her back deck in northern Virginia of a large glass with a straw stuck into what looks to be a substantial margarita]

Me: Happy hour in Lancaster, PA, with about two hundred writers and a mashed potato bar. Pete, Jim says "Hi." [Plus photo of the buffet line and countless options for tarting up a dollop of my favorite food]

Pete: Enjoy.

Dennis: Ahh—a literary smorgasbord.

Me: Nothing like a mashed potato martini...stirred, not shaken...to start the weekend.

Pete: I heard Flaubert only eats the French fries.

Pete: And Joe Conrad hoards the pierogis.

Dennis: Minus the ocean, it looks a little dry.

Brian: Mom and Dad both sound asleep. [Snoring emoji]

Jen: You probably could use a nap now too!

Me: Happy hour at Mom and Dad's?

Brian: [Selfie with a summer ale]

Pete: I'll have what he's having.

That may be the only time one of our texting sessions really was about happy hour.

More likely, one of us has just heard a song on the radio that sets off a chain of memories and messages. Or perhaps one of my amazing nieces or nephews has just done some new marvelous (or marvelously funny) thing. Or (less often) a Philadelphia sports team is having a particularly good day.

Or maybe—and this happens more often that you might think—someone just noticed the time on their watch (or clock, or phone) at exactly 4:41 pm, and that's all it took to reel us all in to a dinnertime conversation.

We're scattered up and down the East Coast now. We see each other and our parents often, but mostly in twos and threes and fours, almost never all at once. Dinnertimes that include all seven of us are rare; if we're lucky, they happen a few times a year.

And yet, without ever talking about it, we've fallen into a pattern of texting our way through the early evening, at what is generally considered the time for happy hour.

These days, if anyone has his or her shirt on inside out, I can't tell. And it's a relief to know a brother can't goose me through my phone. But we've always been able to make each other laugh, and sometimes a thread of text messages is so funny that somebody who reads one at the wrong moment just might snort a little milk (or wine, or beer, or even dinner) through his or her nose.

After all, it's 4:41 somewhere.

About the Author

EILEEN M. CUNNIFFE has undergraduate degrees in English and Honors from Villanova University and a master's degree from the University of Pennsylvania. Her professional career has included roles in healthcare communication, public affairs, the nonprofit arts sector, and higher education—all of which helped her find her voice as a writer. Her earliest essays were first-person travel narratives, but she has also explored identity and experience through the lenses of family, work, and the (part-time) writing life. From 2013–2021, she was a regular contributor to *Nonprofit Quarterly*, covering arts and culture. Her writing has appeared in literary journals and anthologies. Four of her essays have been recognized with Travelers' Tales Solas Awards and another received the Emrys Journal 2013 Linda Julian Creative Nonfiction Award.

Shanti Arts

Nature • Art • Spirit

Please visit us online
to browse our entire book catalog,
including poetry collections and fiction,
books on travel, nature, healing, art,
photography, and more.

Also take a look at our highly regarded art
and literary journal, *Still Point Arts Quarterly*,
which may be downloaded for free.

www.shantiarts.com

www.ingramcontent.com/pod-product-compliance
Lightning Source LLC
Chambersburg PA
CBHW051051230426
43666CB00012B/2646